Robertson

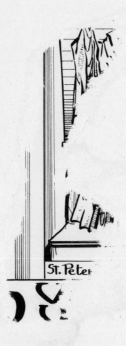

THE EPISCOPAL
THEOLOGICAL SCHOOL
1867–1943

THE EPISCOPAL THEOLOGICAL SCHOOL
1867-1943

BY

JAMES ARTHUR MULLER

Published by
The Episcopal Theological School
Cambridge, Massachusetts
1943

IN
GRATEFUL REMEMBRANCE
OF
WILLIAM LAWRENCE
1850–1941
ALUMNUS, PROFESSOR, DEAN
AND BENEFACTOR
OF
THIS SCHOOL

THE SCHOOL PRAYER

Almighty and everlasting God, who art the only source of light and life; Vouchsafe, we beseech thee, to the institutions of learning in this place the rich gifts of thy good Spirit, that by them all, thy truth may be sincerely sought, effectually received, and obediently followed. Especially upon this school send down the abundance of thy grace that, both in life and doctrine, we may be true followers of thy Son, Jesus Christ, and successful fellow-laborers in the blessed work of setting forward the salvation of all men; and this we beg for Jesus Christ's sake. *Amen.*

"FULL AND COMPLETE"

IN JANUARY, 1896, the Trustees asked Professor Allen to prepare a history of the School. Nine years later he said he was ready to begin. Meanwhile, he had collected some material, and had published two articles on the School in *The Church Militant* (in October, 1903, and April, 1904), but had been busy writing *Christian Institutions* and the *Life of Phillips Brooks*. He asked whether the Trustees desired the history to be "large and full or small and condensed." Robert Treat Paine, President of the Board, said he hoped it would be "pretty full and complete," and the Board voted that it should "deal fully with all matters of interest to the School," but "within the compass of one volume."

This prescription I have endeavored to fulfil, although I have had to deal with the records of twice as many years as Allen would have dealt with had he written in 1905.

He jotted down memoranda of the School's beginnings, especially of the part played in them by Francis Wharton, gathered information about the founder and Dean Stone, collected letters, documents, and pamphlets, and recorded his own recollections and reflections, all of which has fortunately been preserved, although he did not live to put it into shape.

In 1914 Bishop Lawrence, '75, was asked by Faculty and Alumni to write a history of the School for its fiftieth anniversary in 1917. His occupation with the Church Pension Fund prevented his doing so, and J. W. Suter, '85, took his place, producing a lively paper, published in the School *Bulletin* for June, 1917, mainly about the School's early years. It was based on Allen's notes as well as on his own investigations and memories.

In 1926 Bishop Lawrence was again requested to put his hand to the task. He promised to do so. A year later he said, "The bundle of papers gathered by Allen and Suter were transported to my house last autumn, and rested upon my shelves for months as a grim reminder. After conscientious study, I consider that, as with Allen and Suter, my contribution must stop with the early years of the School." The result was a pamphlet, *Beginnings of the Episcopal Theological School*, published as a supplement to the *Bulletin* in July, 1927. It recorded his "personal recollections of the men and incidents of the early days."

In 1940 he produced another pamphlet, *Seventy-three Years of the Episcopal Theological School*, in which he added to his early reminiscences some observations on the School's subsequent history. He had already, in 1926, written a chapter on his own activities as professor and dean in his *Memories of a Happy Life*.

Perhaps it should be noted that when, in the following pages, "Bishop Lawrence" is mentioned or quoted, the reference is to the above named bishop, not to his son.

Although Dr. Drown made no written contribution to the School's history, he talked to the students on the subject annually, and had collected an apparently exhaustless fund of anecdotes about all the earlier deans and professors. Fortunately I made note of some of his talks and many of his anecdotes before his death.

In addition to those who have set out directly to tell something of the history of the School, others have contributed to it while writing of persons connected with it, notably Mrs. Hodges in her life of Dean Hodges, Q. M. Wilder, '42, in his recent degree thesis on Professor H. S. Nash, and C. L. Slattery, '94, in his lives of Professor Allen and E. L. Atkinson, '93, and in his chapters on Allen, H. S. Nash, and Phillips Brooks in *Certain American Faces.*

To all these this book is indebted, as it is to several others who have shared with me or have recorded their memories of life at the School or of those who served it. They are mentioned in the course of the narrative or in the bibliography.

It hardly need be said that I have had access to the School's archives as well as to its publications.

Although it is my hope that all who are interested in the history of the Episcopal Church or in the development of theological education in this country may find much in this book to satisfy them, I must confess that while writing it I have chiefly had in mind the Alumni and other friends of the School. Hence a good part of it partakes of the nature of a family history and will, I trust, be judged in that light.

It was my intention to have it ready in 1942, the seventy-fifth anniversary of the School. I devoted a semi-sabbatical to it and had almost finished it when, at the end of the summer, an unexpected operation laid me up for the rest of the year. This accounts for publication in 1943 as well as for the inclusion of a few matters which earlier completion would have prevented.

At the mid-winter Alumni dinner in 1912 Sherrard Billings, '84, presided. "We older men," he said, "realize, as some of you young fellows do not, that the School in a remarkable way keeps its identity. Almost all of the old masters at whose feet we sat and whom we so much reverenced have gone; and yet the School in an amazing way is the same place. Not only the buildings, but somehow the atmosphere is the same. And it is something that we are grateful for, that it is so."

I have known the School — off and on — only since 1908.

I knew but few of the old masters to whom Billings referred. I never saw Wharton or Stone or Gray or Mulford or Allen or Steenstra. But in reading of the impression they made on those who did know them and, especially, in reading their own letters, I feel that I have come in some measure to know them. I have also discovered, as did Billings, that the School is in an amazing way the same place. And it is something that I am grateful for. I can only hope that in the following pages the young fellows of today will discover that too.

FACULTY PAST AND PRESENT IN ORDER OF APPOINTMENT [1]

Dates include not merely tenure of professorships or assistant professorships, but periods of teaching in any capacity.

FRANCIS WHARTON	1867–81	Dean April–July, 1867
JOHN SEELY STONE	1867–76	Dean 1867–76
PETER HENRY STEENSTRA	1867–1907	
ALEXANDER VIETS GRISWOLD ALLEN	1867–1908	
GEORGE ZABRISKIE GRAY	1876–89	Dean 1876–89
ELISHA MULFORD [2]	1882–85	
HENRY SYLVESTER NASH	1882–1912	
WILLIAM LAWRENCE	1884–93	Dean 1889–93
MAXIMILIAN LINDSAY KELLNER	1886–1922	
EDWARD STAPLES DROWN	1889–1933, 1935	
GEORGE HODGES	1894–1919	Dean 1894–1919
HENRY BRADFORD WASHBURN	1901–02, 1908–40	Dean 1920–40
WILLIAM HENRY PAINE HATCH	1905–07, 1912, 1917–	
PHILIP MERCER RHINELANDER	1907–11	
HUGHELL EDGAR WOODALL FOSBROKE	1908–17	
WARNER FOOTE GOOKIN	1911–17	
JAMES ARTHUR MULLER	1914–17, 1923–	
JAMES THAYER ADDISON	1915–40	
NORMAN BURDETT NASH	1916–39	
ANGUS DUN	1920–	Dean 1940–
SAMUEL McCOMB	1922–26	
WILLIAM LAWRENCE WOOD	1924–25, 1929–36	
CHARLES LINCOLN TAYLOR, JR.	1925–	
RICHARD STANLEY MERRILL EMRICH	1937–	
SHERMAN ELBRIDGE JOHNSON	1940–	
MASSEY HAMILTON SHEPHERD, JR.	1940–	
ADELAIDE TEAGUE CASE	1941–	

[1] For instructors and part time lecturers *see* page 225.

[2] Although Mulford, as a lecturer, was not technically a member of the Faculty, it has long been the custom to include him in Faculty lists.

CONTENTS

THE EPISCOPAL
THEOLOGICAL SCHOOL
1867-1943

I

BISHOP GRISWOLD'S HOPE

THE General Theological Seminary is an institution wise
and useful. I was among the first to bring forward the
motion for its establishment . . . but it causes a loss to this
diocese of some of its most promising young men." So said
Alexander Viets Griswold in 1828. He was Bishop of the
Eastern Diocese, which included all of New England except
Connecticut. He had discovered that men from this region
who studied in New York often stayed there, although des-
perately needed at home. Hence, he said, he hoped for the
establishment of a seminary in New England. Three years
later it looked as if his hope would be fulfilled.

The Eastern Diocese was anomalous in its organization.
Although it met in convention each year, the churches in
each of the states which composed it also held yearly conventions. It was the Massachusetts Convention of June,
1831, which resolved that "There shall be established forthwith by this Convention at Cambridge an institution . . .
to be entitled *The Massachusetts Episcopal Theological
School.*" The Convention proceeded to create a board of
trustees and a board of visitors.

The circumstance which lay behind this action was the
acceptance by John Henry Hopkins of the post of assistant,
on the Greene Foundation, at Trinity Church, Boston.
Hopkins had been rector of Trinity Church, Pittsburgh,
and there had trained theological students in his own home.
Having tried in vain to persuade the Diocese of Pennsylvania to establish a seminary in Pittsburgh, he accepted the

call to Boston on the assurance that one would be established in Massachusetts and placed under his direction.

He arrived in Boston in July, 1831, and in September bought a house in Cambridge "about of a quarter of a mile from Harvard College on the high road to Boston" — presumably Massachusetts Avenue — "sufficiently near to the city to enjoy its benefits and escape its disadvantages." Thus did the Massachusetts Convention, at a time when Emerson was still pastor of the Second Church, venture the perilous conclusion that residence in Boston might have disadvantages.

The Trustees of the new school decided that it was to open on Easter Monday, 1832, and appointed a faculty. Hopkins was to be Professor of Systematic Divinity and have general oversight of the students; Thomas W. Coit, rector of Christ Church, Cambridge, Professor of Biblical Learning; Asa Eaton, of the Boston City Mission, Professor of Ecclesiastical History and Polity; and Bishop Griswold, "Professor of Sacred Rhetoric and the Pastoral Care." [1]

Whether this faculty, other than Hopkins, ever functioned, is not clear; but Hopkins himself did not wait for Easter Monday. No sooner had he settled in Cambridge than he took four students into his house and began instructing them.

Two months later he was asked if he would consider accepting the bishopric of Vermont, which was planning to separate from the Eastern Diocese. He then told the Vestry of Trinity that he would stay in Massachusetts if they raised $10,000 for the Theological School. They replied that they would raise his salary, but do nothing for the School. Concluding that this was an accurate index of the amount of

[1] In the catalogue of the School for 1895–96 it was erroneously said that G. W. Doane, rector of Trinity, Boston, and later Bishop of New Jersey, was one of this faculty. The statement was repeated in subsequent catalogues for thirty-three years. Hence it will doubtless crop up to eternity.

interest in theological education which could be expected from the well-to-do laity, he sent word to Vermont that he would accept. He was elected in May, 1832, and "the Massachusetts Episcopal Theological School," having functioned for one academic year, folded up.

Bishop Griswold was not easily discouraged. In the Massachusetts Convention of 1835 the project was revived and a committee, then appointed, reported in the Convention of 1836 that $22,000 had been pledged; a subscription started in Rhode Island to raise $25,000 for a professorship; and land to the value of $10,000, as a site for the seminary, offered in Lowell, Worcester, Newburyport, Taunton, Northampton, and Pittsfield. As J. W. Suter, '85, remarked: "This geographical display makes an alumnus of today fairly tremble in contemplation of what might have been."

When the Convention heard of these offers, the clergy present said they thought they could raise $38,000 from their parishes in five years, and the Convention as a whole voted to be responsible for $25,000 more. The school was to be opened when $100,000 was in hand. But "the great commercial and mercantile embarrassment," as the Convention, with characteristic moderation, described the panic of 1837, killed the plan.

There was, however, one lasting result of this movement. Miss Betsy Varney, a parishioner of Bishop Griswold at St. Peter's Church, Salem (in those days bishops had to be rectors as well as bishops), died in 1836, and the day before her death made a will leaving $500 for "an Episcopal Seminary in Massachusetts," whenever such an institution should be established. She thus became the first benefactor of the Episcopal Theological School. She appears to have been a person of moderate means; her executor, Dr. George Osborne, who was also her physician, said that she had at one time been an employee of his mother. She died of cancer at the age of forty-seven.

Although the effort to establish a seminary in 1836 was the last to be made publicly in Bishop Griswold's lifetime, the subject was not forgotten. Early in 1839, Professor Simon Greenleaf, of the Harvard Law School, a member of Christ Church, Cambridge, wrote to the Rev. Alonzo Potter, then Professor of Moral Philosophy at Union College, Schenectady, that a seminary was again under discussion. Potter had been rector of St. Paul's, Boston, from 1826 to 1831; he had been a member of the committee which drew up the constitution for the seminary in 1831, and had been chosen as one of its trustees. Shortly after this he had left Boston for Union College.

"A few friends of the plan of an Episcopal Theological Seminary in this state," wrote Mr. Greenleaf, "are still directing some attention to that subject. I have been requested to act with them, but before I decide, I wish, if it be not improper, to know whether you could be induced to take charge of the institution." It was, thought Mr. Greenleaf, a hopeless task to raise money for the erection of buildings and the support of several professors. His plan was to buy "one of the ample mansions" on "the Mount Auburn road," and start with a single professor who would also be rector of Christ Church, "which consists of only about thirty families," but which could pay something toward the professor's salary. A capital of $15,000 would be sufficient, "and this can without doubt be obtained." "I see no hope of success in any other plan; and I cannot bring myself to move in this, without first knowing whether the principal would be acceptable and useful as my parish minister." Presumably Dr. Potter (who was shortly to become Bishop of Pennsylvania) would be acceptable and useful to the thirty families of Christ Church, Cambridge. Potter replied that he saw "very little prospect" of his being able to return to Massachusetts.

Three years later the following entry was made in the diary of William Appleton (great grandfather of William

Appleton Lawrence, '14): "1842. April 15. Went to Cambridge with Mr. Vinton [Rector of St. Paul's, Boston]. Called on Mr. Greenleaf. Much talk as to theological seminary. I said, 'Now is the time to begin; if you gentlemen will put things as they should be, I will purchase the house opposite the Craigie Place, if it is to be had for ten thousand dollars.'"

Bishop Griswold died early the next year, and the Eastern Diocese was dissolved into dioceses named for the states composing it.

Four months before the Massachusetts Convention of 1845, William Appleton and a few other gentlemen met with Bishop Eastburn, Griswold's successor in Massachusetts, to consider, once more, the founding of a seminary. One week before the Convention Appleton went to Cambridge to confer again with Mr. Greenleaf about it. As a result of these conferences, Edward S. Rand (who was to be President of our first Board of Trustees) moved in the Convention of 1845 that a committee be appointed to consider the subject, and in the Convention of 1846 he reported for this committee that William Appleton, one of its members, had pledged $25,000 toward the founding of "the Protestant Episcopal Divinity School of Massachusetts," on condition that another $25,000 be secured within two years.

Appleton wrote in his diary at the time that his proposition "was well received," but expressed doubt that it would be carried into effect. He added, "God will devise all for good."

A numerous committee of laymen was appointed to raise the additional money, but their efforts, if they made any, were unsuccessful. They did not even report at any subsequent Convention. As Bishop Lawrence said, not long ago, "From our present point of view 'God devised for good,' in causing the plan to fall through," for had this, or any of the previous efforts, been successful, the School would have been a local institution under diocesan control.

II

THE FOUNDERS

O NE Saturday afternoon in January, 1867, a wealthy Boston man of business was seized with the apprehension that unless he acted quickly he might not live to act at all. He had, for some time, been thinking of founding a theological school, and this afternoon he put the better part of a hundred thousand dollars' worth of negotiable securities into his pocket and went to see his friend, the lawyer, Edward S. Rand. Meeting him on the street, he thrust the securities upon him, thereby making him, on the spot, the first trustee of the school. He would, he said, shortly make up the amount to the full hundred thousand. Moreover, it was his intention, though he may not have said so at the time, to leave the residue of his estate for the same purpose.

Since it was after business hours, Mr. Rand was obliged "to take the school home in his pocket." He "slept with it under his pillow and sat up with it all day Sunday, never leaving the house."

The donor was Benjamin Tyler Reed.

"I never hear his name read in the Commemorative Prayer," said J. W. Suter, '85, "without reflecting on its rhythmical excellence. If he had been nameless, not even Cranmer could have manufactured out of all Yankeedom a more poetic and satisfying combination of syllables."

Reed had been born in 1801 in Marblehead, Massachusetts, where his family had lived for six generations. His maternal grandfather, Captain John Blackler, raised, equipped, and commanded a company of militia in the Revolution, and had the honor of piloting the boat in which Washington crossed the Delaware. Reed's immediate forebears were importers and ship owners.

He was a classmate of Emerson at Harvard, graduating in 1821. He was not, as he said himself, a diligent student. He partly paid his way in college by teaching in a district school during the vacations. According to his nephew, "He used to say that, feeling his incompetence, he put his scholars back to the beginning of their books, while he studied one lesson in advance each day. He was always very fond of a horse and managed even then to keep one to drive to school and to go to country balls, where, after dancing till nearly daylight, he would often drive to his school in his pumps. But he remembered reproving the girls with whom he had danced if they came to school with their hair in curl papers."

On graduation from college he entered the employ of a ship-owning great uncle, and later went into business for himself, trading with the East Indies and the Pacific Coast. He became an owner of ships and a promoter of railways. He was the first treasurer and manager of the Eastern Railroad, from 1836 to 1847, and acquired interests in other New England roads. In 1847 he became treasurer and chief owner of the Bay State Iron Company, being, as his nephew said, "an enthusiast in the iron business." For many years he was President of the Shawmut Bank. When he was fifty he was heard to say that he had already made and lost two fortunes.

He has been described as "a man of large stature," who "resembled the typical sea captain," yet "of refined sensibilities and a very tender heart." He retained his mental and physical vigor until late in life. Not three years before his death he wrote to his niece that he was about to go up to Conway, New Hampshire, saying, "We don't get our railroad in operation as fast as we expected and I must go there and drive them up. I had hoped, when I became so near seventy, that my days of driving younger men would stop; but in many respects I find myself as young as my juniors."

Bishop Lawrence thus records his youthful impressions of Reed: "He was in appearance the last man to be suspected of interest in theology, the ministry, or the founding of a seminary. . . . He was the picture of a veritable Marble-header; his figure was large and stocky, his face so ruddy that you would have taken him for an old sea dog; with the bluff and autocratic manner of an admiral. I would not have wanted to disobey his orders. . . . He loved a spirited horse, and I see him now in his cutter sleigh trying out the speed of his span against others on the mile course of the Brighton Road.

"Coming nearer to him, one heard beneath his rough voice the notes of tenderness, kindness, and sympathy. He was of that emotional temperament which changes in a moment from the choleric to the sympathetic; generous, high-minded, and daring. . . . He had a high appreciation of culture and sound learning. He had a keen sense of humor, and was a delightful, kindly companion. Above and beyond all these characteristics he was a deeply religious man."

He had been brought up in the Congregational Church in Marblehead, but early in his married life, when living in Boston, became a member of St. Paul's Church. There he remained under the rectorships of John Seeley Stone (later to be dean of the School) and Alexander H. Vinton (later to be one of its instructors). In 1844 he was instrumental in organizing St. Stephen's Church, Lynn, where he had a summer home, and later, when he built a new town house on the outer edge of Boston — at 180 Beacon Street, at the corner of Clarendon — he became interested in the erection of Emmanuel Church. He was elected Junior Warden there in 1863 and in 1869 succeeded his friend Rand as Senior Warden, a post he held till his death.

According to the testimony of both his niece and his nephew, who were raised by him, Reed had long cherished the idea of founding a theological school in Cambridge, but business embarrassments had delayed it.

Dr. Allen (who presumably got the information from Dean Stone) said that when Reed was a parishioner of Stone at St. Paul's, in the thirties, "he lamented to his pastor the consciousness of contradiction under which he lived, devoting himself to the world in order to succeed, while yet desiring to devote himself to God. During many years the plan was maturing of making the great, what seemed to him the only, reparation," namely, "aiding those whose business it would be, unlike his own, to devote themselves to exclusively spiritual ends."

To what extent he was influenced by the earlier attempts to found a theological school in Massachusetts we cannot be sure. He certainly knew of them. He had probably heard Bishop Griswold and Dr. Stone and Dr. Vinton all speak of the subject. Stone had been one of the prime movers in the effort of 1836; had been elected a trustee of the school then in contemplation; and had later written a life of Bishop Griswold, which it is more than likely that Reed had read, in which a theological school in Massachusetts is depicted as one of the Bishop's primary concerns. Vinton had been interested in the effort of 1845–46, and Reed himself had been a member of the diocesan Conventions in those years, when his friend Edward S. Rand and William Appleton led the attempt to establish a seminary. When he told his rector, F. D. Huntington, of his desire to found a theological school, Huntington said that such a school was "one of the foremost wants of the Church in this diocese."

It was to Edward S. Rand, as we have seen, that Reed first turned, as a trustee for his proposed school. Rand, a graduate of Harvard in 1828, was a successful Boston lawyer, active especially in the field of conveyancing. Like

Reed he had been a member of St. Paul's, Boston. In 1860 he had become Emmanuel's Senior Warden. He served as President of the School's Trustees until 1882, two years before his tragic death, when he, his wife, son, son's wife and children all perished on their way to Florida in the wreck of the steamer *City of Columbus* off Martha's Vineyard.

Two other lawyers, Robert C. Winthrop and John Phelps Putnam, were chosen by Reed to act with Rand, and, on January 22, 1867, he signed, with these three, an indenture creating the School.

Putnam, a native of Hartford, Connecticut, and a graduate of Yale in 1837, had studied in the Harvard Law School, practised in Boston, been Judge of Probate for the County of Suffolk in 1857–58, and in 1859 was appointed one of the original judges of the Superior Court of Massachusetts, a post he held till his death in 1882. His early religious training in Hartford had been under Horace Bushnell, but on settling in Boston, he, like Reed, had become a member of St. Paul's. He acted as Secretary of the Trustees until his death.

Robert C. Winthrop, a descendant of John Winthrop, first governor of Massachusetts, had been a classmate of Rand at Harvard. He studied law in Daniel Webster's office, and three years after admission to the bar was elected to the General Court of Massachusetts, where he served six years, the last three as speaker. He was then sent to Congress where he remained ten years, during two of which he was Speaker of the House. On Webster's becoming Secretary of State in 1850, Winthrop was appointed to his seat in the Senate, but lost it the next year when the Massachusetts legislature chose Sumner in his stead. He then withdrew from politics, but later, as Bishop Lawrence said, "came forward as an orator on great national occasions, a representative of the aristocracy of the past, a leader in philanthropic causes, an urbane gentleman, and an outstanding churchman. . . . He was the leading layman in the diocese."

On his eighty-first birthday the *Congregationalist* wrote of him: "He has ever been one of the most loyal, humble, and consistent Christian men among us — one never ashamed of his profession of faith. . . . Men of all denominations rejoice to do him honor." Theodore Lyman, one of his neighbors, wrote to him: "You never neglect a duty and you never forget a friend."

He was a vestryman of Trinity Church, Boston, for sixty years, but he was also connected with St. Paul's, Brookline, where he had a "country home." He succeeded Rand as President of the Trustees of the School in 1882, a position he held until his death in 1894.

Soon after the indenture was signed, the three trustees told Reed that their number ought to be increased to five, and he proceeded to nominate two business men, Amos Adams Lawrence and James Sullivan Amory, who were thereupon elected by the others.

Lawrence (father of Bishop Lawrence, '75) was the son of a wealthy merchant and philanthropist, and, on graduation from Harvard in 1835, went directly into business as a commission merchant. His firm became perhaps the largest distributor of cotton goods in America. He also engaged independently in manufacture, and became the largest producer of knitted cotton fabrics in the country. Like his father, he was a philanthropist. So freely did he spend money and energy in assisting such families to settle in Kansas as would vote to make it a free state that the city of Lawrence in that commonwealth was named for him. Unsatisfied with the Unitarianism in which he had been reared, he began, soon after graduation from college, to attend St. Paul's Church, Boston, during the rectorship of Dr. Stone. At the age of twenty-eight, in the beginning of Dr. Vinton's rectorship, he was confirmed. He became Superintendent of the Sunday School and vestryman. When he moved into the country, in Longwood, he became a vestryman at St. Paul's, Brookline, as he did later at the Church of Our Saviour, Longwood, which he and his brother built in 1867. He was Treasurer of the Theological School until 1883. He served another year as trustee. He died in 1886.

James Sullivan Amory (grandfather of Robert Amory, the present President of the Trustees) was a treasurer of manufacturing companies, a cousin of Lawrence's wife, a resident of Brookline, Superintendent of the Sunday School and warden of St. Paul's there. "He was," says Bishop Lawrence, "a man of great dignity, courtesy, and urbanity." A grandson of James Sullivan, Governor of Massachusetts, 1807–8, "he had a touch of Irish courtesy, never overdone, but a bit finer than that usually found in a Massachusetts gentleman." He served as trustee till his death in 1884, when it was said that "the School could have lost no more faithful or valuable friend." His son, Harcourt Amory, was elected a trustee the same year. Another son, Augustine Heard Amory, '80, the record of whose devoted ministry has been preserved in the *Memoir* by A. W. Moulton, '00, once said: "My father loved his Church and his religion. It was real to him. I don't know any better Christian or anyone whom I want more to be like than my father."

Such was the group of laymen who created the School. They were all members of prominent families, leaders in the professional or business life of their day, two of them, Winthrop and Lawrence, of national consequence. They were also men of religion, neither afraid nor ashamed to be known as such. They were of simple faith, not yet aware of the problems raised by Biblical Criticism. They prayed and read their Bibles, led family prayer in their households, went to church regularly and took their families with them. Their daily activities were distinguished by a high integrity and their use of wealth by a rare sense of stewardship. They were the flower of the Evangelical Movement.

Despite their exacting secular duties, they shouldered responsibility in the diocese as well as in their parishes. Reed, Rand, Winthrop, and Lawrence served as Trustees of Donations; Reed, Rand, Winthrop, Lawrence, and Amory were members of the Committee on the Increase of the Episcopal Fund; Winthrop and Amory were members of the Standing Committee in 1864; Reed in 1865. In the memorable General Convention of 1866, when the Church, North and South, was reunited, the Massachusetts lay delegation consisted of Winthrop, Lawrence, Amory, and Rand.

These men were devoted to the Prayer Book — Reed always carried his with him — and to the Episcopal Church, but were not unready to coöperate with other religious bodies. Said Winthrop: "I am an Episcopalian of the Arnold and Whately school, with something more of the Paley admixture. I agree with Lord Bacon that unity does not necessarily mean uniformity, but if we are to aim at Christian unity, I am not in favor of letting prelatical assumptions stand in the way of it."

Wrote Lawrence: "Of all the denominations into which it [the Church] has become divided, I believe the Protestant Episcopal Church is the best. On that account I joined it nearly forty years ago, and my love of it has increased ever since. But this does not prevent my loving Christians of other denominations and acting with them; and especially it does not prevent my living and acting with those of my own denomination who entertain opinions in which there are 'shades of difference.' "

This last remark is illumined by an entry in Lawrence's diary recording a call on Bishop Eastburn to try to persuade him to deal with the Church of the Advent in a more reasonable manner. When a cross and candles were put on the altar at the Advent, Bishop Eastburn, as Dean Hodges said, "refused to visit the parish for confirmation till the offensive ornaments were removed, and the rector and vestry refused to remove them. Each side exhibited that perseverance of the saints which in sinners is called obstinacy."

Dr. Drown used to illustrate the theological atmosphere at the time of the School's founding by these two incidents:

After Bishop Eastburn had arranged a date for confirmation at the Advent, the senior warden called on him and asked if he would postpone it a few weeks, because by that time a larger class could be prepared. "No," said the Bishop, "the fewer confirmed after instruction at the Advent the better."

At Grace Church, Newton, while Peter Henry Steenstra was still rector, the Bishop, when vested and about to enter the chancel, noticed two vases of flowers on the altar. "Mr. Steenstra," he said, "although I know that you make no idolatrous use of these flowers, I cannot, on principle, take part in a service with them on the Holy Table." Steenstra replied that since the congregation was already in the church it would look queer if he went in at that time and removed the flowers. He suggested that they both go in to begin the service and immediately kneel at opposite ends of the altar, and, while the congregation had their eyes closed in prayer, reach up and each take a vase from the top of the altar and put it underneath. To this the Bishop agreed, and this they did!

Services in most of the Episcopal churches in and around Boston, at the time of the founding of the School, were conducted with the utmost simplicity, as they had been since colonial days. In Morning and Evening Prayer the minister faced the people continuously. At the Holy Communion he stood at the north end of the altar. That sacrament was administered but once a month, on the first Sunday, but it was preceded by a preparation service the evening before, so that the communicants came to it "religiously and devoutly disposed."

Bishop Lawrence used to say that when he was a student in college no clergyman, as far as he knew, wore either a cassock or a colored stole. They wore long surplices, reaching to the ankles and opening down the front, and changed, for the sermon, into black gowns with white neck tabs or "bands." The first wedding he conducted after his ordination in 1875 was in a church which had introduced colored stoles. He knew nothing about them, and as the rector was not there to explain, he concluded that the gayest was the most appropriate for a wedding and wore red!

Into this New England simplicity the Church of the Advent had projected disturbing novelties, disturbing especially to Bishop Eastburn. There were not only candles and a cross, there was Holy Communion every Sunday and saint's day; the clergy consecrated the elements with their backs to the people; at Morning and Evening Prayer they faced across the chancel; they turned toward the altar in creeds and glorias; they preached in surplices instead of gowns; and they had a vested choir and processional hymns. "I recall," said Bishop Lawrence, "going as a boy to the Church of the Advent to see Mr. Henderson, the grocer, dressed up in a white gown in the choir."

Although Bishop Lawrence's father and his fellows deprecated the extreme attitude of Bishop Eastburn and may have been willing to let the Church of the Advent go peacefully on its way, they did not want to follow in that way themselves. They had little sympathy with the Oxford Movement or with the Ritualistic Movement which followed it. In one of his earliest communications to the Trustees Reed wrote: "It is my anxious desire that in appointing professors they should be selected from the Evangelical class, who believe in the doctrines of the Church as declared at the Reformation. . . . I would by all means avoid the appointment of men who would magnify the forms of the Church above its teachings, or who would imitate any of the ceremonies of the Papal Church."

Reed and his associates all numbered clergymen among their close friends. Reed's niece said, somewhat quaintly, of him that "he truly loved all men but especially children and ministers." A continuous stream of clerical visitors flowed through the Lawrence house in Longwood. In the character of the clergy with whom they were intimate these laymen were fortunate. Most, if not all, of them had been confirmed by perhaps the greatest saint who ever ministered in New England, Bishop Griswold. At St. Paul's, Boston, Reed, Rand, Putnam, and Lawrence had sat under John Seeley Stone, "very gentle in his manners and full of graciousness," and his successor, Alexander H. Vinton. Daniel Webster called Stone the ablest preacher he had ever heard, and Phillips Brooks characterized Vinton's ministry as "the strongest and most effective which our Church has ever had in Boston." When Reed and Rand became members of Emmanuel Church their rector was Frederic Dan Huntington, previously professor at Harvard, subsequently Bishop of Central New York. And when Winthrop, Amory, and Lawrence went to live in Brookline and the others visited them, there at St. Paul's was Francis Wharton, one of the most remarkable men of his time.[1]

It was a ministry exemplified by men such as these that Reed and his associates hoped to perpetuate and increase when they organized a school in Cambridge.

[1] Stone was rector of St. Paul's, Boston, 1832–41, and of St. Paul's, Brookline, 1852–62. Wharton succeeded him in Brookline, 1863–71. Huntington was rector of Emmanuel, 1860–69. Vinton followed Stone at St. Paul's, Boston, 1842–58, and Huntington at Emmanuel, 1869–77. Bishop Eastburn was rector of Trinity, 1843–69. A statement made by Bishop Lawrence, in *The Church Militant*, May, 1920, that the pastors of Reed and the original Trustees all advised against placing the School in Cambridge needs modification. Both Wharton and Huntington favored Cambridge. Stone did not. I have not come upon an expression of Vinton's or the Bishop's view.

III

WHARTON AND THE CONSTITUTION

O<small>F THE</small> clergy with whom Reed and the Trustees were intimate the one who exercised most influence on the formation of the School was Francis Wharton. Indeed, so great was his influence that Dr. Allen regarded him as the real founder of the School. "He often imparted to me," said Allen, "his relations with the origin of the School. . . . He was profoundly interested in theological schools and it had been his ambition to be connected with one. . . . He had studied the working of the institutions at Gambier, Philadelphia, and Virginia," and noted what he felt to be their limitations. To him, said Allen, Reed entrusted the task of drawing up the School's constitution.

Francis Wharton was born in Philadelphia in 1820. His father was of Quaker ancestry, but had accepted a captaincy in the army in the War of 1812, had married an Episcopalian and become one himself. Graduating from Yale in 1839, Francis Wharton thought seriously of preparing for the ministry, but being dissuaded by his father, studied law in his father's office. At the age of twenty-six he published a treatise on Criminal Law which passed through nine editions during his life, and was so enlarged in the process that it was broken into three separate works — *Criminal Law*, *Criminal Evidence*, and *Criminal Pleading* — in five thick volumes. So ably was this work done that *Criminal Pleading* achieved a tenth edition in 1918, *Criminal Evidence* an eleventh in 1935, and *Criminal Law* a twelfth in 1932. In addition to this, he published four other legal treatises during a decade of successful practice, during part of which he was assistant to the Attorney General of Pennsylvania.

After the death of his wife in 1854, he gave up his practice, became editor of the *Episcopal Recorder*, and, two years later, Professor at Kenyon College.

Allen was a student at Kenyon at the time and found Wharton his most stimulating teacher. "I gained from him," said Allen, "a lasting interest in literature. He was by constitution a humanist with an instinctive perception of the quality and meaning of life, with a deep sympathy for all human manifestations. He made all he touched interesting. From him I gained my first conception of the picturesque aspects of history, and my first conviction of its value as a psychological revelation of the soul of humanity."

Though still a layman, Wharton became a leader in the religious life of the college. Said Allen, "The same fascination and sense of the living reality of things he carried into his work as a lay-preacher. I recall the crowds that flocked to the basement hall of Rosse Chapel to listen to his lectures on the Acts of the Apostles. It was no ordinary man who could have drawn students from their rooms or people from their homes on those winter evenings, as he did for successive weeks, to such an uncouth, ill-ventilated, badly lighted room."

In 1862 at the age of forty-two he was ordained, and the next year called to the rectorship of St. Paul's, Brookline, which he held till 1871, although from 1867 he combined it with service to the School.

On April 19, 1867, the Trustees appointed him Dean of the School, an office which he occupied eleven weeks, resigning on July 3 in favor of Dr. Stone.

In 1859 he had published a book of theology entitled *A Treatise on Theism and on the Modern Skeptical Theories*. In 1867 he published another called *The Silence of Scripture*. He would have liked to have taught theology at the

School, and was appointed professor of it by the Trustees, but with characteristic self-effacement ceded that chair, as well as the deanship, to Dr. Stone. He was able, however, to exercise his theological talent in courses on "Evidences of Christianity" and "Apologetics." In addition, he taught Liturgics, Polity, Canon Law, Homiletics, and Pastoral Care! "He could lecture in an interesting way on almost any subject," said Bishop Lawrence, throwing in pleasant anecdotes, dryly humorous quotations, kindly advice, and "hunks of wisdom drawn from experience."

Despite his legal learning he was not greatly interested in Canon Law. It was Apologetics in which he delighted. As Dr. Allen said, "His conception of Christianity did not emphasize its legal aspects." In the State law was important, but "in the Church lay the sphere of that higher freedom where law passes into the glad performance of duty." Moreover, Canon Law had been for much of its history a restriction on Christian liberty.[1]

In addition to his varied duties at the School Wharton lectured on International Law at Boston University and produced eight more legal treatises, including one on International Law which won instant recognition on both sides of the Atlantic. He saw through the press at least a dozen revisions and enlargements of his earlier books.

An affection of the throat which gave his voice a high falsetto quality, amusing to the students, finally made it almost impossible for him to speak at all. Hence he resigned in 1882. In 1885 he was appointed Chief of the Legal Division of the Department of State in the first Cleveland administration. In addition to his duties in this office he compiled, at the request of Congress, a three volume *Digest of International Law* and a six volume collection of *The Revolutionary Diplomatic Correspondence of the United States.*

---

[1] He did, however, write an able monograph on American Canon Law for W. S. Perry's *History of the American Episcopal Church* (II, 390).

He was reading the proof sheets of this when he died in 1889. The eleventh edition of the Encyclopaedia Britannica calls him "the foremost American authority on International Law." Incidentally, he and William Lawrence are the only men who have served on the Faculty to whom articles in any edition of that work are devoted.

Besides numerous articles, his books include a score of titles in some thirty volumes, several of which are of staggering proportions. Few of his law treatises contain less than 750 pages to a volume and there are frequently two or more volumes.

John Bassett Moore, who knew Wharton in his last years in Washington, said that "he possessed in the highest degree vivacity of intellect"; "the activity of his mind was incessant"; he had "quickness and breadth of comprehension," an exceptional memory, an almost unlimited capacity for work, and a sparkling humor. There were, said Moore, humorous passages even in his treatise on Criminal Law. As a jurist he was interested not in legal technicalities but in broad principles of justice.

He was indeed a man of astonishing versatility and incredible industry. When in Brookline, he wrote his sermons so far in advance that at one time he had accumulated fifty which he had not yet preached. When the Rev. W. Wilberforce Newton visited him one Saturday night in 1869, he found him writing a funeral sermon, correcting the proof of a law article, and reading a law book all at once! "His remarkable habit of doing two or three things at the same time," said Newton, "surprised me greatly." Wharton surprised his students in Cambridge by correcting proof before, after, and sometimes during class.

Having entered the ministry late in life, he never lost the lay point of view. This, combined with his clear judicial mind, peculiarly fitted him to be the adviser of Reed and his colleagues.

The unique features in the organization of the School were due to him; namely its independence from the control of any ecclesiastical person or board or convention, and the wholly lay composition of its Board of Trustees.[2]

"It was Dr. Wharton's conviction," said Dr. Allen, "that the School, separated from any organic relation to the diocese, would thus escape the gusts and flurries of partizan feeling to which ecclesiastical conventions are liable." Said J. W. Suter, '85, "Wharton feared the results of control by the clergy and most of all by bishops, or worst of all by one bishop." "Students of theology," said Bishop Lawrence, "as well as those of philosophy and science must always be intellectually ahead of the average, and if in theology a man is ahead of the average he is liable to be dubbed a heretic by the average and pulled back, with the result that theological study, if it is linked up with any diocesan organization, is liable to drop back to the commonplace." "Those who planned the foundations of this School decided that laymen, who did not necessarily know theology, would be better administrators of a theological school than bishops or clergymen who, knowing something of theology, might in their differences forget to notice the more important things." "The system has worked well for sixty years, and I believe will work well."

That it has worked well not only for sixty years but for seventy-five has been due, as Wharton may have anticipated, to the willingness of the Trustees, as laymen, to entrust to the Faculty, as clergymen and teachers, the theo-

[2] The Fundamental Articles do not specifically say that the Trustees must be laymen, merely "members" of the Episcopal Church, but, as the Trustees said in 1885, when the question was raised (see below, p. 67), the founder had chosen only laymen and had "exhibited and expressed so decided a preference for having laymen only" that no change in this respect had ever been contemplated. The charter originally limited the number of Trustees to five. This limit was increased by legislative enactment to seven in 1889, nine in 1913, and eleven in 1922.

logical and academic direction of the School. As Dean
Hodges once observed, the relation of the Trustees to the
Faculty has, in practice, paralleled that of a vestry to the
clergy of a parish: the Trustees look after the temporalities
and leave the spiritualities to the Faculty.

One feature of the coöperation of Trustees and Faculty
rightly impressed Dr. Allen. "The great reason for the success of the School," he said, "is that the Trustees, in making
appointments, have conferred with the professors until
unanimity has been reached. Harmony and freedom have
thus been secured. Those who know theological seminaries
are aware of the evil that reigns where this harmony is lacking."

Although the Faculty were to be free from control by
other theologians or would-be theologians, the Fundamental
Articles provided that the bishop of the diocese together
with three clergymen and three laymen, appointed by the
Trustees, were to have an advisory oversight of the School
as a Board of Visitors. "No bishop," said Dean Hodges in
1906 (and it is equally true today), "is more influential in
the counsels of any diocesan institution than is the Bishop
of Massachusetts in the direction of this School, and his
influence is all the more sought and valued because it is our
privilege rather than his prerogative."

Another provision of the School's Fundamental Articles
is that in order "to secure a reasonable degree of independence," the professors shall hold their positions during good
behavior and be subject to removal by the Trustees only
on trial. "To this point," said Allen, "Dr. Wharton attached
the highest significance. Incapacity must be proved and
demonstrated. Of course it hurts an institution to accu-
mulate dead weights, incompetent men. But it hurts more
when they are dismissed in any arbitrary fashion." It should
be noted that this virtual permanence of tenure applies only
to those members of the Faculty who hold the rank of pro-

fessor and to them only after they have served an initial
appointment of three years.

That one of the School's Fundamental Articles which
may not be changed provides that instruction shall be in
conformity with the doctrine, discipline, and worship of
the Episcopal Church and shall "embody and distinctly set
forth the great doctrine of Justification by Faith alone in
the Atonement and Righteousness of Christ as taught in
. . . the Thirty-nine Articles, according to the natural con-
struction of the said Articles (Scripture alone being the
standard) as adopted at the Reformation, and not according
to any tradition, doctrine, or usage prior to the said Reformation, not contained in Scripture."

As Dr. Drown so often pointed out, the doctrine of
Justification by Faith might have been identified with some
special dogmatic theory and the emphasis on the supremacy
of the Bible might have been tied to a mehanical doctrine of
inspiration. But phrased as it is, this theological provision
of the Constitution has permitted the essential content of
these principles rather than a narrow interpretation of their
letter to be expressed in the teaching of the School. "The
principle of Justification by Faith in Christ," said Drown,
"has emphasized the Person of Jesus as the heart and centre
of Christian faith and of Christian life. The principle of the
Supremacy of Scripture has emphasized the fact that the
Bible is the supreme source for our knowledge and understanding of Christ, and that it therefore demands thorough
and critical study, unhampered by theories put upon it from
outside."

As already noted, the indenture containing the School's
Fundamental Articles was signed on January 22, 1867. The
Charter or act of incorporation is dated June 1, 1867. In
the former the title of the School is "The Protestant Episcopal Theological School of Massachusetts," and this is the
title used in the first issue of the Catalogue. In the Charter

the institution is called simply "The Episcopal Theological School," and the second and all subsequent issues of the Catalogue so designate it.

The deletion of the words "of Massachusetts" was undoubtedly done to remove even the suspicion of subordination to the diocese. It is not so easy to account for the dropping of the word "Protestant." It may have been due to Wharton's essential catholicity. It may represent merely the desire for a less cumbersome title.

In addition to Wharton's influence on the Constitution of the School, it was he who nominated Dean Stone and the rest of the original Faculty. Moreover, he backed up Reed and the Trustees in their intention to put the School in Cambridge, and he raised $12,000, chiefly from friends in Philadelphia and New York, to purchase the ground on which the School Chapel stands — the first part of the present School property to be acquired.

Not the least of his contributions to the School was his own comprehensive spirit, rare in those days of partizanship. He was wont to point to "the tolerant and Catholic platform which the Anglican Communion adopted at the Reformation." "Our Articles," he said, "were meant as the symbols of peace and comprehension. They were broad enough at one time to shelter the supralapsarian Calvinism of Archbishop Whitgift. They were broad enough at another time to shelter the mild Arminianism of Secker and Tillotson. . . . Whenever we have deviated from this policy our glory and our power have been proportionably diminished. It was by the application of the doctrine of compulsory uniformity that we lost the passionate eloquence of Whitefield, the sagacious sense of Wesley. . . . Through it we lost something more — the works and examples of those great confessors, the Puritan Divines of the Restoration, who in their exodus spoiled us of the jewels and wealth of an orthodoxy which we were too indifferent to appreciate, and of a literature whose depth and fullness we were too luxurious and inert to fathom. . . . There go John Bunyan, and Baxter, and Owen . . . and there [Milton] taking with him as he goes from this his mother church, the glory of the greatest epic poet whom the world ever knew. What, indeed, might the Church not have been had her heart been as comprehensive as her standards!"

He maintained that parties in the Church were not only a sign of the Church's vitality but also of its perpetuity and unity. They were called into being by the need for emphasis on neglected phases of truth. If they ignored the truths which other parties stood for, they might become less than Christian, but on the whole they had shown a tendency to learn from each other and enrich the common heritage. He expressed the hope that the Evangelicals would "not become less evangelical," but "more and more sacramental, more and more impressed with an appreciation both of the ethical and of the institutional sides of the faith, more and more loyal to the Catholic creeds, and more and more fearless in appealing to reason."

At the fiftieth anniversary of the School in 1917 there were reminiscences of Francis Wharton. Reuben Kidner, '78, described him thus: "He was short and not by any means slender. He had a peculiar gait, like the roll of a sailor in a storm. It was beautiful to see him going down Brattle Street with his overcoat pockets stuffed, as they always were, with proof sheets. He was always correcting proof sheets." Recalling the custom of those days of wearing long surplices opening down the front, with no cassock beneath, Kidner told how the students made merry over Wharton's appearance in chapel with his surplice gaping wide and "a very emphatic bay window" protruding from the gap.

Bishop Lawrence remembered him "rolling up Brattle Street with a watermelon under each arm." "It became a tradition in Cambridge about stout Dr. Wharton and his two watermelons. In fact he was a character." The Bishop as a boy had sat regularly in a pew near the pulpit in St. Paul's, Brookline, while Wharton was rector. "It was my habit," he said, "to take my Sunday School library book into Church and read throughout the service. One Sunday morning as Dr. Wharton met me on the steps, he said, 'Willie, it would help me very much if you would not read during the service, the turning of the leaves disturbs me, but you may begin to read at the sermon.'" He was, said the Bishop, "a kindly featured, plump, cheery man, with a high voice, delightful smile, bright eyes, and quizzical humorous look. He suffused cheer and kindness." On coming to Cambridge, he continued to be "the same hospitable, sweet, humorous, pious, charming, rotund personality."

He was a lover of dogs. In Brookline he was seldom seen without a huge St. Bernard, which occasionally followed him into church for service. One day in Cambridge a small and very dirty Skye terrier attached itself to him on his way to the School. When the class of '78 went into the recitation room they found Dr. Wharton and the terrier, the latter dripping wet and shivering, the former saying, "Poor doggy! Poor doggy!" "When we entered," said Kidner, "he looked up and said, 'Oh, gentlemen, I have caught a dog. I took him down in the cellar and let the tap run on him, and he seems very cold and wet. What do you think I ought to do?' Barrington [a member of the class], having an alert mind, suggested that the dog ought to be taken home at once. The dog was taken home at once — and we had the same lesson for next time."

This not too pleasant tempered animal became so devoted to the Doctor that it accompanied him regularly to class and sat beneath his table, keeping a malevolent eye on the students. By making faces at the beast, C. M. Addison,

'82, could start it barking vociferously, to the divertisement of his classmates and the puzzlement of their teacher.

Six years after his wife's death Dr. Wharton had married again. He frequently entertained the students in his home. But when the hands of the clock approached nine he would remark to his wife: "Won't it be lonely, dear, when all these young men have gone home in half an hour!"

As Kidner said, "He was a great man, and because he was an amusing man we should not be sorry. . . . He was the intellectual founder of the School."

There is a sentence in his *Silence of Scripture* which he himself exemplified: "The oars of Providence are muffled. We know not our hour; hence we are to labor as if we were to live forever, and trust as if we were to die to-night."

IV

BEGINNINGS

Among the clergy whom Reed had consulted about the proposed School was his rector at Emmanuel Church, Frederic Dan Huntington. Dr. Huntington said emphatically that the School ought to be placed in Cambridge. Its board of trustees, he suggested, should consist of the bishop and the Standing Committee of the Diocese — a suggestion which, as we have seen, was not accepted, thanks to Francis Wharton. On the character of the faculty Huntington, who had himself been a professor at Harvard, gave this pertinent advice: "Obscure men will not do. Small men will not do. One-sided men will not do. There must be exemplary piety, unquestioned ability, unimpeachable learning, and a large style of manhood." These qualities, he said, were essential in Cambridge, "where the genuineness, the thoroughness, and the comprehensiveness of a teacher's mind would be likely to be subjected to more trying tests" than anywhere else in the country. That the school might win the confidence of the Church generally, he urged the appointment of "moderate men, holding Evangelical views clearly and intelligently, yet holding them in a comprehensive spirit and with a conciliatory temper."

The first man called, Professor L. W. Bancroft of Bexley Hall, threw cold water on Mr. Reed's plan. Energies should be concentrated on the schools already in existence, he said; there was no need for another, particularly not in Cambridge; "the moral atmosphere there is not healthful"; theological students need "to be withdrawn for a season from the world."

Next Phillips Brooks, then in Philadelphia, was sounded out. If he would come he could take whatever professorship he liked as well as the deanship. He said he felt that he ought to stay in parish work. "I am not made for a professor," he added.

On his refusal, Francis Wharton accepted the deanship and the chair of Systematic Divinity, both of which he shortly ceded to John Seeley Stone, but not before he had gathered a faculty. It was probably Wharton who had suggested calling both Bancroft and Brooks. It was certainly he who nominated Stone and the rest of the Faculty. Wharton's intention, at first, was to retain his rectorship in Brookline along with his work at the School; there were to be three other lecturers, also engaged in parish work, and two resident members of the Faculty, Dean Stone and A. V. G. Allen. Allen, who had been a student under Wharton at Kenyon College, had graduated from the Andover Seminary two years before and was, at the time, rector of St. John's Church, Lawrence. He was to be Assistant Professor of Ecclesiastical History. Frederic Dan Huntington was asked to be lecturer in Pastoral Theology; Henry Codman Potter, assistant at Trinity, Boston, lecturer in Homiletics and Polity; Peter Henry Steenstra, rector of Grace Church, Newton, lecturer in Hebrew and Greek Exegesis. Huntington declined; he said he was already overworked. Potter and Steenstra accepted, but Potter resigned in the spring of 1868, when he was called to Grace Church, New York. It is improbable that he did any teaching before he left.

In 1869 both Allen and Steenstra were made Professors, Steenstra with the title of "Professor of Hebrew and Biblical Criticism and Interpretation," which was shortly expanded into "Professor of Biblical Interpretation, including Criticism and Exegesis of the Original Text, and Acting

Professor of Oriental Languages with Biblical Antiquities Annexed." It is small wonder that he no longer had time or energy for his Newton rectorship. He came to live in Cambridge in 1869. Wharton, who taught everything no one else did, resigned his rectorship and moved to Cambridge in 1871.

These four men, Stone, Wharton, Steenstra and Allen, did all the teaching during Stone's deanship.

In addition to gathering a faculty, the Trustees had the task of securing grounds and buildings, and the money for them; for Reed's gift of $100,000 was for endowment. Temporary quarters for the School were found in two frame houses on the south side of Mount Auburn Street near Mount Auburn Cemetery. One faced Elmwood Avenue. To it came Dr. Stone in October, 1867, and waited for students to arrive. The other, on the corner of Coolidge Avenue, just across from the cemetery, was to be the School. "Skeptics," said Bishop Lawrence later, "averred that the School would soon move into the cemetery." In this second house were to be class room, students' quarters, chapel, and rooms for Allen, who was to act as "house father." Allen delayed his coming from Lawrence till there was reasonable prospect of at least one student.

The first public service in the improvised chapel was conducted by Dean Stone on the third Sunday in Advent, December 15, 1867. This, in a sense, was the opening of the School. On the previous Monday the Dean had written to Mr. Rand: "Dr. Wharton has sent a lectern and four settees and a lot of Prayer Books, but we shall need six or eight more settees." He evidently expected a few dozen worshippers. How many came we do not know. The first student did not appear until New Year's Day.

"Dr. Stone wrote me," said Allen later, "about the middle of October that three students had been heard from, but he was not sure that they were coming. We waited a little longer, and in the middle of November he wrote me that a student was plainly in sight. So about the first of December, 1867, I came to Cambridge and took rooms in the house on Mount Auburn Street. There I waited for a month, and no student came. It was on the first day of January, 1868, and it was at four o'clock in the afternoon that a student by the name of Sylvester — from Danvers — presented himself. I remember well the day. It was a dark winter afternoon and rather cold. We had a large fire in the open grate, and at four o'clock he came into the study and sat down, and we talked over Church history. That was the opening of the Theological School."

The student was William Wallace Sylvester, later rector and builder of the Church of the Advocate, Philadelphia.

In 1868 a part of the present site, on Brattle Street, was purchased. Almost next door stood — as it still does — Craigie House, the fine colonial mansion of the poet Longfellow, used in revolutionary days as Washington's headquarters; round the corner was the elm under which Washington took command of the American armies, and the common on which the "embattled farmers" from Lexington and Concord had encamped; down the street in one direction was the "spreading chestnut tree" of the village blacksmith; up the street in the other, the house of James Russell Lowell; directly across, John Fiske, the historian, later came to live. Harvard University was then a small institution with some five hundred undergraduates and about as many graduate students, most of them in medicine and law.

The widow of the late Dean Briggs of Harvard has recorded her memories of Harvard Square at the time: "It was like the square in a country town. Near where the subway entrance now is there were hay scales, and not far away — half way to Dunster Street — was a big elm tree (out in the street) with a curb around it on which were kept the red wooden buckets that were used to water the horses of the 'Union Railway Company' — that road ran from Harvard Square to Bowdoin Square where it ended. Those horse cars were funny little cars with no ventilation on top, and in cold weather they had straw on the floor to keep our feet from freezing on the half-hour trip to Boston."

Bishop Lawrence was an undergraduate at Harvard from 1867 to 1871, during the first years of the School's life. "As I looked out of my college window," he said fifty years later, "I watched the farmers, who had driven their loads of cord wood and hay from the north, and were selling them under the elm in the centre of the square." He recalled the neighborhood of the School in those early days: "Few streets, none in this country, had more dignity, beauty, and historic interest than Brattle Street. Across the river in open view were the hills of Brookline and Brighton, and the masts and sails of the schooners moving up and down suggested scenes of Holland. The street was then a winding, shaded road, the uncurbed sidewalks melting into the roadway; the great colonial houses, unsurpassed in simplicity and true proportions, were surrounded by ample grounds. One almost looked for the Tory owner with velvet coat, short clothes, and periwig, to come down the path. Instead, there walked leisurely down the steps of Craigie House terrace Mr. Longfellow, who as he came upon the roadway met Mr. Lowell. Longfellow with long, snowy beard and hair, benevolent in look; Lowell in natty jacket with jaunty air.

"The atmosphere of Cambridge was charged with culture, self-satisfaction, and mild or militant Unitarianism. The culture and literary charm the people of the whole country admired: the Unitarianism the people of the whole country west of the Berkshire Hills misunderstood and abhorred."

The first building to be erected was the Chapel, the gift

of Robert Means Mason, son of the jurist, Jeremiah Mason, and cousin and business partner of Amos A. Lawrence. He was interested in the School from its inception and served on its first Board of Visitors. He and Lawrence were, next to Mr. Reed, the most munificent of its early benefactors, his benefactions, including $75,000 for the Chapel, amounting to some $110,000.[1]

He was, said Robert C. Winthrop, Jr., noted "for scrupulous integrity, combined with singularly sound and accurate judgment. . . . Profoundly attached to the Anglican Communion in which he had been educated, he was catholic enough to recognize a bond of fellowship with the upright and devout of every creed. . . . He belonged to what, by some mysterious dispensation, seems destined to become an almost extinct type of churchman — one whose regular attendance on public worship is the conscientious discharge of duty to his Creator, however uninteresting the service and however dull the sermon."

His life was "one of great material prosperity, coupled with an unusual succession of domestic sorrows," namely, the deaths, at intervals over a period of sixteen years, of his only son, his wife, two of his daughters, and his brother, the Rev. Charles Mason, rector successively of St. Peter's, Salem, and Grace Church, Boston. In their memory he built the Chapel.

The plans of the architects, Ware and Van Brunt, were accepted in the spring of 1868, the corner stone laid in July, and the completed building consecrated as St. John's Memorial Chapel on November 16, 1869. At that service there were present two notable young men: Phillips Brooks, who only two weeks before had become rector of Trinity Church, Boston, and Charles W. Eliot, less than one month

[1] To this his daughters added about $30,000. The gifts of Amos A. Lawrence and his wife amounted to about $120,000. Their son, Bishop Lawrence, contributed some $50,000 more.

President of Harvard, who, as Bishop Lawrence remarks, must have found Bishop Eastburn's wordy sermon dull.

Some years later Bishop Clark of Rhode Island said he once asked Bishop Eastburn why he gestured so violently when he preached, since it often left him physically exhausted. "I have to," replied Bishop Eastburn, "to conceal the poverty of my thought." "I'm not sure," added Clark, "that he always succeeded."

Dr. Drown was present when this was told, as was President Eliot. It was the only time, said Drown, that he ever saw President Eliot laugh.

St. John's Chapel was intended to be not only the chapel of the School but also a center of Church life for the academic community in Cambridge, for Christ Church was then making little impression on the College. There were Sunday services in the Chapel, morning and evening, and seats were reserved for Harvard students. Until 1885 their attendance at some church on Sunday was compulsory, and a hundred or more came regularly to St. John's. They continued to do so for several years after compulsory attendance was abolished. The rest of the seats were soon filled by neighboring residents. The preacher was normally the Dean, but for seven years after the Chapel was opened, on the third Sunday evening of each month, it was Phillips Brooks. Then camp stools filled the aisles; the doorways were thronged; people came an hour before service to get seats.

One day in the early years of the School, Longfellow met Dean Stone in front of the Chapel and said: "I never pass your grounds and this Chapel without thinking of the words of the benediction in the Prayer Book, *The Peace of God, which passeth all understanding.*"

Later he wrote:

> I stand beneath the tree, whose branches shade
> Thy western window, Chapel of St. John!

And hear its leaves repeat their benison,
On him whose hands thy stones memorial laid. . . .
Not only tongues of the Apostles teach
Lessons of love and light, but these expanding
And sheltering boughs with all their leaves implore,
And say in language clear as human speech,
"The peace of God, that passeth understanding,
Be and abide with you forevermore."

The tree mentioned in this poem was an aged hybrid walnut-butternut said by Professor Charles S. Sargent of the Arnold Arboretum to be one of only five or six known specimens. Under it the June meetings of the Alumni were held for many years. After much propping-up it came down in 1929. Ten years before, William H. Lincoln, President of the Trustees, had planted near it an oak which has taken its place as the Alumni Tree.

In 1869 the houses on Mount Auburn Street were given up. Dean Stone moved into the house at the corner of Mason Street and Phillips Place. It had been bought by some of his friends and given to the School on condition that he occupy it till his death.[2] A large, square, wooden dwelling, no longer standing, on Brattle Street at the corner of Irving Place (now Brown Street) was acquired for the School.

Said John Bacchus, '73, recalling his student days, "Together with Dr. Allen, who was then unmarried, we occupied a roomy frame house with pleasant grounds about it just down Brattle Street from the School grounds. In that house we lived as a family. There we lodged, there we ate, there we studied, there we recited." When Bacchus was a Senior there were ten students in the School. "We were a small family," said Dr. Allen. "The School existed in poverty and obscurity and amid much opposition, but no family was ever happier than we were in those early years."

[2] Since occupied by Professors Allen, Kellner, McComb, Norman Nash, and Taylor.

With surprising rapidity buildings essential to the School went up. The architects of the Chapel were commissioned to draw a plan for the School quadrangle, and in 1873 the first unit of it, a dormitory for twenty men, as well as the ground upon which it stood, was presented to the School by Amos A. Lawrence. This was the half of Lawrence Hall nearest Brattle Street. The founder, before his death in 1874, gave $25,000 for a library. This, with the addition of $10,000, raised by the Trustees, paid for Reed Hall, which was completed in 1875. "Its architecture," said the School Catalogue, "is somewhat unique"! "Its style," commented the *Boston Herald* of July 18, 1875, "with the little tower rising from the centre of the front roof, is not easily described." "The little tower" was blown askew by the hurricane of 1938 and, to the joy of Dean Washburn, removed. The building contained class rooms and offices in addition to the library, which was housed in the large central room on the second floor, now known as Paine Hall.

Three years before the completion of Reed Hall the books of the Rev. John Singleton Copley Greene, a member of the Board of Visitors, were left to the School. Before the School took possession of them they were destroyed in the great Boston fire of 1872, and the School received $10,500 insurance, the income from which has continued to the present to supply a welcome fund for the purchase of books.

The School, comparatively well-off in buildings, was not receiving sufficient income from its endowment for running expenses. In April, 1870, Dean Stone reminded the Trustees that it was three months since he had received from them any money to pay servants and workmen. "It is," he said, "not only unpleasant to my feelings but repugnant to my principles to employ this class of people without making them prompt and regular payment. I beg you, therefore, to excuse me from acting any longer as the Dean." Presumably the money was forthcoming for the Dean continued to be Dean. In 1875 he wrote: "Every new building adds to our expense for fuel and ground-dressing and general care. Boarding house, dormitory, library, and lecture rooms eat up coal like an ocean steamer."

To meet this difficulty something very like what we have imagined to be a recent invention came into existence. Annual contributions to current expenses were sought, and those who gave were spoken of as "Friends of the School." During the first six years of the School's life almost $27,000 was contributed, the largest givers being the Rev. J. S. Copley Greene, Amos A. Lawrence, Robert Means Mason, and Dr. Wharton. James S. Amory was the most active of the Trustees in raising this money. Dr. Allen said the School must have closed had it not been for the "constant efforts of Mr. James S. Amory," and "the strong assistance of Mr. Amos A. Lawrence."

Bishop Lawrence in 1927, referring to this early period, said, "Professors and alumni of today have no conception of the poverty of the School and the financial limitations under which the work was done. I can recall my father saying again and again, 'James Amory has done his best in begging; I can advance no more money; unless something happens the School must close its doors.' . . . This impecunious condition continued from the foundation through the years when I was Dean, and into Dean Hodges' time, when upon the death of Mr. Reed's widow, who had a life interest in a large part of his estate, the endowment was enlarged.

"She was much younger than he, being a second wife. When Dr. Stone made his first call of condolence upon her after Mr. Reed's death, she exclaimed, 'Now, Doctor, don't you wish I were dead?' At which he responded in his sonorous voice, 'O Queen, live forever!'

"She acquiesced."

Knowing of the School's urgent needs, Mr. Nathan Matthews, a wealthy member of the Church of the Advent, Boston, donor of Matthews Hall and the Matthews Scholarships at Harvard, wrote to the Trustees on February 26, 1873, that he was desirous of promoting sound theological learning through the School at Cambridge. But the School should, he said, "fairly and adequately represent the Church as a whole, and not be the organ or instrument of any party. . . . Its teachings should conform to the standards of the Church as they are generally accepted. . . . To this end its Trustees and Faculty should be composed of gentlemen who, while otherwise qualified, can fully represent the great body of Churchmen. Should you agree with me in these views, and are willing to act upon them, I should be ready to give to it the sum of one hundred thousand dollars. . . .

"It is my earnest wish that this institution shall be the leading divinity school of our Church, and Cambridge has greater advantages than any other location for such a school."

The Trustees asked him to state his desires more explicitly. He replied: "Inasmuch as there are different parties [in the Church] and as the High Churchmen outnumber the others, I would suggest, as an equitable and satisfactory arrangement, that the Board [of Trustees] consist of two Low Churchmen and three High Churchmen, two of whom should be conservative. . . . If such a Board is selected, I hope the terms High and Low Church may be forgotten in the future management. . . . There is a belief on the part of the High Churchmen that the institution, as now represented, is under the management of the Low Church party."

The answer of the Trustees, dated March 31, 1873, was composed by Robert C. Winthrop, and, according to the Memoir written by his son, he took some pride in it:

"You are right in thinking that the institution under our

charge is greatly in need of additional funds. . . . And it is with the deepest regret that we have found ourselves unable to accept at once the munificent provision which you have offered. . . .

"We are happy to agree with you that it is necessary to the success and efficiency of any such school that 'it should fairly and adequately represent the Church as a whole, and not be the organ or instrument of any party.' . . . You must pardon us, however, if we are unwilling to admit that there has been anything in the management of the School at Cambridge, thus far, which is inconsistent with this acknowledged principle. We should certainly be unjust to the able and accomplished professors who are in charge of the institution, were we ready to acquiesce in the idea that their teachings have not 'conformed to the standards of the Church as they are generally accepted and understood by the great body of our clergy and people.' . . .

"But the conditions of your proposal, we are aware, relate primarily to the composition of the Board of Trustees . . . that a majority of the present Board should vacate their places, as coming within your understanding of Low Churchmen; and that three Churchmen, who should have approved themselves as High, and two of whom should be conservative as well as High, should be elected to the vacancies. And from such an arrangement you hope there may be harmony in the Board, and that the terms High and Low Churchmen may hereafter be forgotten.

"For ourselves, we prefer to forget these terms now. . . . They are nowhere found in the standards or formularies of the Church. They are applied very much at random, sometimes in ignorance and sometimes from prejudice. . . . They are the last terms we desire to recognize in the organization or management of the institution. The differences which they are employed to indicate vary with the varying hour. We should hardly know how to define them in their simplest form; but when you add 'conservative' to 'high,' and require two of the three High Churchmen to be conservative also, we should be entirely at a loss to find an arbiter for deciding upon such qualifications. . . .

"But it cannot be supposed that the changes you have suggested are to end with the reconstruction of the Board of Trustees. Your remarks that 'the teachings of the School should conform to the standards of the Church,' can have reference only to the professors. You would thus seem to contemplate the substitution of other professors in place of those who now occupy the chairs of the seminary. We should be unjust to the faithful men who, with very insufficient remuneration, have conducted the institution through the difficulties and discouragements of its infancy, if we were to subject them to the risk of being displaced by a new Board of Trustees. It would hardly be an alleviation of our compunctions at having assented to a course which might involve such consequences, to know that we had done so under the temptation of a large increase of our resources. If any changes are to be made in the organization or management of the institution, we venture to think that they should be made upon their own merits, and not in consideration of an endowment, however liberal, or however needful. . . .

"We thank you for your generous proposal to aid it [the School], and cordially unite with you in the wish that it may still become one of the leading divinity schools of our Church. We had hoped that your bounty might have contributed to such a result. And it is with sincere regret that we find ourselves constrained to decline the conditions with which your offer is accompanied."

V

DEAN STONE

JOHN SEELEY STONE became dean at the age of seventy-two. He was two years older than was Dean Washburn when Dean Washburn retired! Like Dean Washburn, he was, at that age, still vigorous in mind and body. J. G. Bacchus, '73, remembered him as "a man of commanding presence, erect as a statue."

When Bishop Lawrence was an undergraduate at Harvard there was a tradition, which he believed to be a fact, that one day when Dr. Stone "was walking in front of College House, a Harvard student, as he thought, insulted a girl, and the Dean knocked him down." "It did more good," said Lawrence, "for the Episcopal Theological School than many lectures."

That Dr. Stone was chosen dean was due primarily to his position of leadership among the Evangelicals. His connection with the School would win confidence for it among those who feared that the rationalism and Unitarianism of Cambridge might corrupt its theology. Indeed Dean Stone himself was one of those who thought it was a mistake to place the School in Cambridge.

He had been born in western Massachusetts in 1795 — Great Barrington, West Stockbridge, and Berkshire are all said to have been his birthplace. In 1814 he had shouldered his musket and marched to the defense of Boston against the expected attack of the British. He graduated from Union College in 1823 and studied theology at the General Seminary. After short periods of teaching at Hobart College and ministering in Maryland and Connecticut, he served as rector of St. Paul's, Boston, for nine years (1832–41), of Christ Church, Brooklyn, New York, for eleven (1841–52), and of St. Paul's, Brookline, Massachusetts, for ten (1852–62), where he preceded Wharton. In his prime he was regarded as one of the greatest preachers in the Church. Moreover, it was said of him that "his presence in the pulpit was in itself almost a sermon, for he was a singularly handsome man and gifted with a most winning address."

Either in Boston or in Brookline or in both places he had come into intimate contact with the founder of the School and all five of the Trustees. They all had the highest possible regard for him and fell in at once with Wharton's suggestion that he was the man to be dean. He was not without academic experience, for he had, on leaving Brookline, become a lecturer in the then recently established Philadelphia Divinity School, whence he was called to Cambridge. He was likewise an author of some standing, having published lives of Bishop Griswold and James Milnor as well as five volumes of lectures and sermons.

"He was not a skilled administrator," said Bishop Lawrence, "nor an inspiring teacher, but his gracious presence, friendly temper, and solid piety were of great value in those early days." Said Dr. Allen: "Dean Stone taught Pearson on the Creed and Burnet on the Thirty-nine Articles, and when the boys were not ready to recite he was only too ready to recite for them."

From the testimony of all who knew him, he appears to have been a straightforward, transparent, lovable, and somewhat absent-minded old gentleman, who not infrequently invited friends to dinner and then forgot it and went off himself to dine elsewhere. One of his acquaintances turned the tables on him by appearing occasionally, uninvited, at dinner time and enjoying the Doctor's apologies for having forgotten that he had invited him. He was a veritable father to both students and Faculty. Steenstra spoke of him as "our grand old Doctor." Allen became his son-in-law in 1872.

He was deeply saddened by the defection, in 1869, of his son Kent to the Roman Church, and this doubtless increased his fear of Romanism and Tractarianism. On the other hand, he opposed what he called "the rationalistic tendencies of our time," and meant the School to stand as a bulwark of Evangelicalism.

In 1873 he wrote to his friend Dr. Heman Dyer, of New York, who had heard disturbing rumors of the School's heterodoxy: "Our course of study is thoroughly orthodox and our professors are highly Evangelical — some of them would perhaps be called hyper-Evangelical" and "somewhat more than quasi-Calvinistic"! "Our position here in Cambridge is a trying one, unwisely chosen as a *place* for a school of theology; and then our Church throughout the land is more than cold towards the institution. . . . But here we stand, and by God's help we will make the best we can of our position, few and weak though we are as a faculty."

The first Catalogue of the School announced that as soon as the endowment was sufficiently enlarged it was proposed to have five resident professors, one for Oriental Languages and Biblical Archaeology, one for Biblical Criticism and Interpretation, one for Systematic Divinity and Apologetics, one for Ecclesiastical History and Polity, and one for Homiletics, Pastoral Care, and Liturgics.

These subjects, it went on to say, comprehend "a full and liberal course of Theological, Ecclesiastical, and Practical Study; and such a faculty, of earnest able men, sustained by a sufficiently ample endowment . . . and pervaded by the true spirit of Missions, Sunday Schools, and practical Church work, would be able to conduct the institution with large efficiency."

It was long before the resources of the School could support five professors, but, as already noted, the four original teachers all soon became resident, and although we do not know if they were all "pervaded by the true spirit of Sunday Schools," there is no doubt that they "conducted the institution with large efficiency."

The school year was divided into three terms, ending respectively at Christmas, Easter, and Commencement. At the end of the third term there was "a public examination of all classes, conducted by the Faculty in all the studies of the year." This examination was oral, each professor taking a different day in the week before Commencement. Trustees, Visitors, neighboring clergy and their congregations were invited to attend. The most regular in attendance were the Visitors, including the Bishop, and the Massachusetts canonical examiners, who, in Bishop Eastburn's time, accepted the results in lieu of canonical examinations.

The major studies ran through the three years, namely Hebrew and the Old Testament in that tongue; the New Testament in Greek; Church History, including History of Doctrine; Theology, including Evidences and Apologetics. Liturgics, Polity, Pastoral Care, and Homiletics were given one or two terms each. There was little change in this pattern for twenty years.

According to the first Catalogue, "Absences shall be noted at every recitation and a report thereof annually made by each professor to the Board of Visitors." What the Board of Visitors were to do about it was not said. After 1873 the matter was left to the Faculty.

Expenses for the school year, exclusive of books, clothes, and travel, were estimated, during Dean Stone's time, at $250 a year. The cost of board and washing oscillated between $4.50 and $5.00 a week. As was the custom at other seminaries, there was no charge for tuition or room rent. But life at Cambridge was more expensive than at other seminaries, because of the School's lack of scholarship funds, a condition periodically complained of by the Dean.

Family Prayers (from the back of the Prayer Book) were said daily by Mr. Allen, the House Father, in the house temporarily occupied by the School until January, 1872, when the School began to use the Chapel for daily Morning and Evening Prayer, led by each professor in turn for a week.

There was a weekly "Faculty Meeting" attended by both Faculty and students. This was alternately a "devotional evening spent in prayer and simple religious conversation," and a homiletical exercise, in which the Faculty criticized student sermons. These "Faculty Meetings" are not mentioned after 1872, but in 1874 a weekly devotional meeting, led by a member of the Faculty, was instituted.

In that year the students petitioned for a weekly Communion during Lent. Dean Stone in his reply to them said that "the Faculty thought it desirable that the Dean should lay the matter before the Bishop, as President of the Board of Visitors, and be in some measure guided by his advice." On doing so they found that Bishop Paddock, who had succeeded Bishop Eastburn in 1873, "considers the general practice, which confines the administration of the Lord's Supper to the first Sunday of every month and to the three Great Festivals, Christmas, Easter, and Whitsunday, a happy medium between a too frequent and a too infrequent repetition of that sacred ordinance." Nevertheless, the Faculty, feeling "a most tender sympathy with the piously expressed wish of the students," will administer the Communion thrice in Lent and once a month during the rest of the school year, on Wednesday mornings.

During Dr. Stone's deanship the student body seldom numbered more than a dozen, the largest enrollment coming in his last year (1875-76), when there were fifteen regular and two partial students. That the School was already attracting men of sound preliminary education is evidenced by the fact that one of the partial students and twelve of the regulars had college degrees. Five were from Harvard, two from Kenyon, two from St. Stephens, and one each from Bowdoin, Brown, Dartmouth, and Wesleyan.

There was, in Dean Stone's days, a student association, meeting weekly, "for improvement in composition and elocution," named after the founder, *The Reed Brotherhood*, which, we are told, somewhat enigmatically, "merged into an Association of Alumni" in 1874. This was the beginning of the Alumni Association.

The first public commencement of the School was held on June 21, 1871. There had been no graduating class in 1870. The Chapel had not been completed when the class of 1869 finished the course, and the School had no place to hold a commencement for them. Hence in 1871 the three graduates of 1869 as well as the two of 1871 received degrees.[1]

In 1872 a class of six was graduated and each one of them read an essay at the commencement exercises, a custom fortunately abandoned three years later. This commencement of 1872 was made memorable, as Dr. Allen said, "because Mr. Reed was present for the first time, to witness the fruition of his desire. He sat in an armchair placed for him on the right side of the choir, facing the congregation. He sat alone, receiving in his humble way the honors due to the founder of the institution. . . . Throughout the service there was a look on his face of profound satisfaction, of deep inward serenity and happiness. He never came again." He died March 29, 1874, having made the School the residuary legatee of about half a million dollars. Since, however, his widow, his son, and his son's wife had life interests in it, it was long before it came to the School.

[1] W. W. Sylvester, the first student to enter, was given his degree in 1885, as of 1868.

Nevertheless, the news that the School would some day receive it put heart into the Faculty. Wrote Allen, "We had been depressed a good deal," but now "are feeling very hopeful." "Never in the history of the American Episcopal Church has such a gift been made before, and that, too, without any condition whatever. We shall soon, I hope, begin to make ourselves felt as an institution. I do not know when we shall begin to feel the change in our salaries."

Another notable occasion, according to Allen, in the first decade of the School's life, was the visit of Charles Kingsley in 1874. He was the guest of Dr. Wharton, and Allen spent an evening at Wharton's with Kingsley and Longfellow. Kingsley had been overworked and was nervous and irritable, "but under the influence of Longfellow's gentleness and the genial manner of the host, he gradually mellowed." Wharton had promised him exemption from speech making, but wanted the students at least to see him, so he took him to chapel next evening and introduced him to them. Kingsley "broke his intention to be silent, making an address which those who heard will never forget." He referred to the Prayer Book as a bond of unity among English-speaking peoples, and to his pleasure in hearing its familiar language so far from home, and then went on to "the thought that there was one thing which it was always becoming to say, under any circumstances to any audience, educated or uneducated, students for the ministry or for any other profession, which should be the lodestar of their theology and of their lives — *He hath showed thee, O man, what is good; and what doth the Lord require of thee, but to do justly, and to love mercy, and to walk humbly with thy God?*"

Bishop Eastburn was always friendly to the School. At his death in 1872 he left it his library and an estate of $23,000, which came to it after his wife's death. His successor, Bishop Paddock, was suspicious of the School's orthodoxy. He wrote to Dean Stone in 1875 suggesting that the School make an annual report to the Diocesan Convention. The Dean replied that this had never been done because it was the wish of the founder "to secure the institution from falling under the control of the Convention and thus to keep it from ever being embroiled in the strifes which so often agitate conventions." "The only objection, so far as I can see," said the Dean, "to making the report rises out of the tendency of *custom* to grow into a claim of *right*; first a claim of right to *demand* such report; and finally a claim of right to control the institution thus reporting itself."

The Trustees hastened to back up the Dean, saying, "We are all of us opposed to putting ourselves or the School in the hands of the Convention, or recognizing or impliedly admitting that it has any right to inquire into or be informed of our doings."

Three years later, in his address to the Convention, the Bishop said: "Official cognizance of all religious work carried on in the diocese is not my privilege; for to be invited, with all one's neighbors, to see and hear, is not quite a churchly recognition of a bishop's office. A bishop cannot so far forget his office as even to seem to give *official recognition* to agencies which, largely occupying themselves with the teaching of doctrine and worship, nevertheless distinctly disallow any Episcopal interference with or supervision over the religious teaching in vogue. . . . But I shall not dwell on so painful a topic as a bishop's enforced declaration of irresponsibility for Christian work within his own diocese."

He advised his candidates to go elsewhere for their training.

From the first, Harvard assumed a most cordial attitude toward the School. In 1866, before it was known that Mr. Reed intended to found the School, the Methodists were considering establishing a seminary somewhere in the neighborhood of Boston, and Edward Everett Hale, in the name of the Overseers of Harvard, wrote, on December 15, to the trustees of the proposed Methodist institution, urging them to place it in Cambridge.

"The Corporation," he said, "renews the statement, which it has frequently made on all proper occasions, that it will gladly extend to any theological institution of whatever Christian denomination the privileges and opportunities which it has extended to the various professional schools now connected with the University." These privileges were the use of the libraries and museums and admission "without charge to all the lectures known as university lectures, and to all the courses of lectures, properly so called, delivered to the undergraduates." He added that the University would reciprocally profit by "an enlargement in the means of the study of theology and a consequent enlargement in the religious influences of Cambridge upon a thousand young men assembled there."

On the same day, Hale wrote to Richard Henry Dana, Jr., telling him about his letter to the Methodists and adding: "I cannot but think that the measure would be advanced and the cause of religious learning as well, if *at this time* gentlemen in the Episcopal Church were willing to move for a foundation at Cambridge for a theological school. That would show the Methodists that they need fear no trap on our Unitarian side, and it would stimulate the Corporation also."

Dana forwarded Hale's letter at once to Reed, saying: "I have not answered Mr. Hale's note and shall not name your plan to him, as I consider it a secret."

What Reed replied to Hale we do not know, but it is certain that despite those Episcopalian advisers who, like the Methodists, feared the Unitarian trap, he concluded that the advantages of Cambridge as a situation for his school and the opportunity it offered as a center of Episcopal influence outweighed its drawbacks.

No sooner had the University learned of Mr. Reed's appointment of trustees than E. R. Hoar wrote to Mr. Rand in behalf of the Corporation, saying: "We shall be happy to do anything in our power to forward your enterprise." This was on February 11, 1867. On October 1, 1868, Andrew Preston Peabody wrote to Rand: "The Corporation of Harvard College will be most happy to give to your Theological School a beneficial connection with the University and to assign to it the same place in the annual Catalogue which is given to the professional schools immediately under their control." He went on to say that Episcopal theological students could be put on the same footing as resident graduate students in their use of the library and museums and attendance at lectures, and concluded: "It cannot be without a decided influence on the many undergraduates from your Church who are looking to the ministry, that they shall have become familiar with your School through the annual catalogue; while we shall rejoice in the strong and salutary influences, which cannot but flow from your School and its Chapel services for large numbers of our pupils."

This hearty welcome, as well as the University's previous eagerness to have the Methodist seminary in Cambridge, may be accounted for, at least in part, by a circumstance not mentioned by Dr. Peabody. The Harvard Divinity School, although in theory non-denominational, was, in personnel, Unitarian, and in consequence Harvard, as a whole, had the reputation of being "a Unitarian college." Outside of New England — indeed outside of eastern Massachusetts — Unitarianism was not looked upon with much favor, and Harvard, because of this, was failing, in comparison, for instance, with Yale, in drawing students from other parts of the country. Hence any connection, however tenuous, which it might claim with a theological school of another name than Unitarian would be of distinct advantage. Small and weak as the Episcopal School was, its mere existence in Cambridge was of advertising value to the University.

The University Catalogues from 1868 to 1886 contained a section devoted to the School of exactly the same nature as the sections devoted to the Medical School, Law School, or other graduate departments. Beginning with 1879, there was a note that the School was "not a part of the organization of Harvard University," but prior to that date there was nothing to lead the uninformed reader to suppose that the School was anything but a part of the University. Had the reader looked at *The Harvard Directory* for 1873-74 or *The Harvard Index* for the same year, his impression would have been confirmed.

In February, 1870, a full page advertisement of the University appeared on the back cover of the *Atlantic Monthly*, *Harper's*, and three other periodicals. It began by mentioning the number of teachers and students at Harvard "divided among the following departments." Then came brief descriptions of these departments, among which was the Episcopal Theological School. President Eliot wrote to Dean Stone that the School's share of the advertising costs was $100, but added, "As you know, the School was not consulted as to the time and manner of this advertisement, and therefore is under no obligation whatever to pay anything." The Dean cannily suggested that since the University paid rent to certain Cambridge churches for pews occupied by its students, the free pews for such students in St. John's Chapel might be considered as an offset to this charge.

As for the University's advertisement, no one reading it could have divined that the School was not a department of Harvard. As a matter of fact many people thought it was. One of the press accounts of the School's commencement in 1871 began: "The first Commencement of the Episcopal

Theological School of Cambridge, which is a constituent part of Harvard University, took place on the 21st." Dean Stone wrote with concern to Mr. Rand: "I find that in some public prints, particularly in *The Nation*, we are put down as a constituent part of Harvard University. Is this in accordance with the views of our Trustees?"

If, as Dean Stone thought, the School was suspected of Unitarianism and rationalism because it was situated in Cambridge, how much more, if it were believed to be a part of Harvard. The Trustees, however, do not appear to have been so fearful of this as was the Dean, and although the School was not thereafter advertised in the periodicals as a department of Harvard, a section of the University Catalogue was, as we have said, devoted to it for several years. As late as 1889 *The Churchman* spoke of the School as "one of the Harvard group of institutions."

Not only did Dean Stone feel that the Unitarianism of Harvard gave the School a sinister, if undeserved reputation, he was convinced that the neighborhood of Boston was bad for the students. In his report to the Trustees in 1874 (the first such report to be made), he lamented the temptation which "proximity to a large city holds out to the indulgence of a natural fondness for the theatre, the opera, and social amusements generally. . . . Late hours are sure to postpone the study of next day's lesson till the small hours of the night; and then come *late rising*, absence from chapel, and a disturbing tardiness at meals."

Early in 1875 he was distressed by another matter which had nothing to do with the location of the School. "One of our students," he wrote in desperation to the Trustees, "keeps a huge dog in his room. I have required the removal of the dog repeatedly, yet in vain. And as the dog has become an intolerable nuisance, injuring the building by his urine and excrements and making the corridors noisome by their odor, I should advise the expulsion of both student and dog. Before taking any disciplinary step, however, I have thought best to lay the case before you."

As soon as the student heard that he had been reported to the Trustees he got rid of the dog.

When the Dean reached the age of eighty he began to think of retiring. George Zabriskie Gray, rector of a flourishing church in a New Jersey suburb of New York, was proposed as his successor. The Dean wrote to his friend, Dr. Dyer, for information about Gray: "Is he a sound Churchman, without obnoxious extremes in either direction? Is he a good business man? Would he do more than I have done in attracting general confidence in our School? In answering this last query, don't be tender on my account; I am old and tough and can bear without wincing anything that *you* will say."

Dr. Dyer replied that Gray was an excellent business man; a successful rector, getting people of all shades of churchmanship to work harmoniously together; a wide reader, "never brilliant, but always interesting"; "his fairness toward those whose opinions are different from his own is almost remarkable"; "he is not widely known, but wherever known he inspires respect and confidence." "He is not Dr. Stone. Nor is any other man Dr. Stone. This may be a misfortune, but it is nobody's fault."

Gray was called to take over the deanship after Easter, 1876, to be pastor of the Chapel congregation, and to relieve Wharton of the teaching of Homiletics and Liturgics. To these duties there was added, after his arrival, that of Acting Professor of Systematic Divinity.

Concerning the Chapel congregation Stone wrote to him: "In Cambridge the Episcopal element is not superabundant. . . . New England people are not given to any easy shifting of pastoral relations, yet they are much given to running after extra services. When Mr. Brooks preaches the Chapel is always crowded, sometimes to overflowing, with university students and people of all denominations."

He closed the letter with a word of welcome, masterful in its tactfulness: "In coming from New Jersey to Massachusetts you will, I doubt not, become conscious of a change. . . . The people of Boston are slow in forming a judgment of a new comer, but if they find him a true man, they adopt him as one of themselves and stand by him through *thick and thin*. For yourself, as an expected stranger, I have no fear. You will come among us quietly, as we await you; take up your work modestly, as it meets you; and do it earnestly, as God gives you strength; and gradually you will find hearts warming to you, and yourself in an assured position of credit and usefulness, which I pray you may long hold and fill."

Dean Stone continued to live in the house at 2 Phillips Place until his death in 1882 at the age of eighty-seven. Phillips Brooks wrote to a friend at the time: "I saw him about two weeks ago, and he was lying on the sofa in his study as cheery and full of fun as ever. . . . It was a beautiful old age and death."

The Faculty resolutions on that occasion summed up admirably his service to the School: "He brought with him a name and influence. . . . How deeply he inspired the confidence of those who had called him is revealed in the munificent endowments and in the noble array of buildings which he was privileged to witness. . . . The generous donors of these gifts had all of them at some time come under his influence. . . . He was revered for his simple piety, his unquestioning faith, his large minded spirit, his manliness, his tolerance, his gentleness, his unfeigned humility."

Said the Trustees, "His dwelling among us has been as a benediction."

Dr. Drown used to delight to tell how one day Dean

Stone's little granddaughter ran to him, knelt down beside his armchair, and said: "O grandfather, I do so want to be a Christian."

"Well, my dear," replied the Dean, "I don't see the slightest objection."

VI

DEAN GRAY, THE SCHOOL, AND THE VISITORS

GEORGE ZABRISKIE GRAY became dean in 1876 at the age of thirty-eight. He was born in New York City in 1838 of well-to-do parents and baptized in the Dutch Reformed Church. His parents, moving to Staten Island and finding neither Reformed nor Presbyterian Church near them, connected themselves with the Episcopal Church at Clifton. There George Zabriskie was confirmed while in his junior year at New York University. He graduated in 1858. He was an excellent linguist, having, as a boy, spent some time at school in Geneva, Switzerland. On finishing College he travelled for a year in Europe and the Near East. Theology he studied first at Alexandria and, after the Civil War broke out, at Philadelphia. After brief ministries at Vernon, New Jersey, and Kinderhook, New York, he served as rector of Trinity Church, Bergen Point, New Jersey, for eleven years (1865–76), whence he was called to Cambridge. He had already declined calls to the Philadelphia Divinity School and to Bexley Hall. He was the author of four small books, two before and two after his coming to the School.

Being a New Yorker, he was not always appreciative of Boston — in spite of Dean Stone's tactful admonitions. "He had a pretty hard time," said Bishop Lawrence, "and so did the professors — for a few years. He poohpooed at everything that was dear to New England." When he read the tablets at Lexington which tell how many redcoats so and so shot from behind this stone wall, he exclaimed: "Just like them, the cowards! Kept behind a stone wall!"

In his *Memories* Bishop Lawrence recounts an incident illustrative of the pleasant provincialism of Cambridge, which, he says, Dean Gray never quite understood: "The Misses Palfrey were typical. One autumn upon their return to Cambridge, Dean Gray said, 'Have you had a good summer, Miss Palfrey, and where have you been?' 'We have had a delightful summer. We stayed at a great hotel in Magnolia, and met a number of really intelligent and agreeable people of whom we had never before heard.' "

Although Dean Gray was an Evangelical, he came to appreciate and to share other points of view. Bishop Lawrence said of him: "Dogmatic in manner, he was in fact receptive of new truth. Strongly set in argument, he would feel the truth in the reasoning of the other side, and in time would unconsciously absorb what he had denied in debate. He gradually allowed himself to breathe more and more the atmosphere with which he was surrounded."

His position, as it came to be under the influence of Cambridge and the School, is accurately described in the Faculty resolutions at the time of his death, in which it was said that he "united in a singular degree conservative devotion to essential Christian truth with an open eye and receptive mind for new thought and the best methods of theological teaching."

In his first years his own teaching consisted of hearing recitations — on Van Oosterzee's Dogmatics, on Pearson on the Creed, on Browne on the Articles. To the class of 1882 he assigned the memorization of the Thirty-nine Articles in Latin. When, under the leadership of C. M. Addison, the class rebelled, he compromised on having them memorized in English! Later he was less tied to the text book, but, as Bishop Lawrence said, "He was not a scholar but a reader, and he threw his somewhat undigested conclusions at the students, sometimes in such a way as to confuse or stun them, and when they asked Dr. Allen what the Dean meant he was unable to tell them."

He was, however, an administrator with a keen sense of business, a faithful pastor of the Chapel congregation, and a hospitable friend of the students, many of whom found a second home in the deanery which he built and which was given by his widow to the School. C. M. Addison recalls playing hide and seek in the deanery and the Dean racing wildly down the stairs in order to reach base before being caught.

"There was," said Bishop Lawrence, "behind his strong mind and frame, his brusque and sometimes aggressive manner, a heart as tender as a child's. . . . His emotional nature was very near the surface; . . . he unconsciously covered it with this thin shell of an abrupt manner."

Dr. Drown, who was one of his students, used to say that he hid an affectionate, sensitive disposition under a somewhat pompous and bombastic exterior. Drown recalled how one day in class a hurdy-gurdy struck up just outside the window. The Dean wrathfully flung up the sash and sternly ordered the organ-grinder to depart, which he did. Returning to his chair, the Dean, instead of proceeding with his lecture, sat silent, his face growing redder and redder as he thought of the crestfallen Italian slinking off in silence. Up he rose, again flung open the sash, called back the retreating musician and pressed a coin into his hand. Dr. Drown added that he was sure that if the Dean could have done so without the class seeing it, he would have given the man a banknote instead of a coin.

The change in the School's administration is noticeable in the first issue of the Catalogue under Dean Gray. The previous issue had covered twenty-four pages; this thirty-two. Now for the first time a picture of the School appeared. And a great deal more was made of the School's situation in Cambridge. Dean Stone's misgivings about Cambridge have been noted. In the Catalogues issued during his administration access to the College library was mentioned and in the early issues it was said that "the society of this our most ancient seat of learning is quiet, cultivated, and refined, and is as favorable as can anywhere be found to habits of patient and thorough study." But even of this Dean Stone was not sure. The sentence ceased to appear after 1872.

Dean Gray's first Catalogue opened with the statement that "the School was established in this city because its founder felt the importance of a seminary in so great an educational center." It would remind young men who were studying here of the claims of the ministry, and "benefit the Church at large, by both representing it in such a center" and by "the training of a thoroughly educated ministry." "The School is now ready to invite to its halls candidates from all dioceses who desire to pursue their studies in the university town of America."

Chief among the advantages of Cambridge are "the opportunity and stimulus afforded by the proximity to a great university and by free access to the libraries. . . . It is the aim of this School to improve these advantages to the utmost, so as to send into the ministry men of generous culture and wide sympathies, qualified to handle the questions of the day and to meet the peculiar demands of the time."

"The situation is in all respects convenient, and the heart of Boston may be reached in thirty-five minutes. The Watertown and Mount Auburn horse railways pass the School, having their terminus in Bowdoin Square, Boston." [1]

C. J. Palmer, '78, recalls that when he was a student at the School "Oliver Wendell Holmes, Longfellow, Charles Eliot Norton, Andrew Preston Peabody, President Eliot,

[1] Electric cars replaced horse cars in 1889. The subway was opened in 1912.

James Russell Lowell were to be met on the horse cars any day. Cambridge was then much smaller than it is now and all these men were well known and helped to make the atmosphere. . . . The Longfellow girls were in high school and their aunt, Mrs. Greenleaf, was always present at the daily services in the seminary Chapel."

Early in Dean Gray's administration the quadrangle of the School, as originally planned, was completed, by the erection of the refectory in 1879 and of the second half of Lawrence Hall in 1880. The refectory, built at the cost of $12,000, came as the result of a direct appeal from the Dean to John Appleton Burnham, a member of St. Paul's Church, Brookline, and a cousin of Mrs. Amos A. Lawrence. He had made a fortune in cotton and railroads and had previously given $15,000 toward the purchase of the School property. The second half of Lawrence Hall, like the first, was the gift of Amos A. Lawrence, the whole costing about $85,000. The deanery, built by the Dean himself, was finished in 1879.

The Dean had a card headed "Rules for this Building" tacked up in each room of Lawrence Hall. These rules would be welcomed by some present-day occupants, but others would regard them as an abridgment of Christian liberty; for instance: "Musical instruments may not be used in the rooms without permission"; "Singing and all disturbing noises are to be avoided in the hall-ways." One is illustrative of the living conditions of the time: "Lamps must be filled in the day-time, when there is no danger from other lights."

Along with the increase in physical equipment, deficits for current expenses continued, although Dean Gray's exceptional business acumen reduced these expenses to a minimum. "If any theological seminary is managed more inexpensively," he wrote to Amos A. Lawrence in 1878, "I should like to know it"; and in 1882, "What a happy

day and what a new sensation when there will be enough
on hand to pay the School's debts!" The next year the
Bay State Iron Company, in which the School was a share-
holder through Mr. Reed's bequest, failed, resulting in a
loss of $6500 from the School's capital fund. In 1883 the
friends of the School were appealed to for an annual "Income Deficiency Subscription," and during the five and a
half years ending in October, 1889, contributed $44,500.

In 1879 what are doubtless regarded by many as recent
innovations, namely, certificates and general examinations,
were introduced. For graduation, all who passed "the ordinary examinations" were to receive a certificate and be
enrolled among the Alumni. For the degree of B.D. a man
had to pass "an especial examination covering the studies
of the whole course" and present two theses. After 1884
one thesis was sufficient.

The Faculty explained to the Trustees that the certificate
would free them "from a constant conflict between kindness and duty," for they had not infrequently recommended
men for the degree "on the score of charity" — a weakness
not unknown among their successors.

Despite stiffened requirements for the degree, the enrollment increased. In Dean Gray's first year there were
fourteen students, in his last there were thirty-six. This was
the more significant, said the Dean, when it was considered
that "this is the only seminary, as far as is known, that offers
no scholarships. Every year there are many desirable applicants who are compelled to go elsewhere because of our
inability to give the aid that other institutions offer." He
noted, however, with satisfaction in 1886 that of the 141
students who had been enrolled since the School opened,
forty-nine had come from other seminaries, while only
three had left to study somewhere else.

This increase was due to various causes: a fuller use of
the printed word in describing the life and aims of the in-

stitution; the enthusiasm of the Alumni for the School; the growing reputation of some of the Faculty — Allen's *Continuity* appeared in 1884; some notable additions to the Faculty, to be mentioned later; Phillips Brooks' friendship for the School; and, paradoxically, the opposition to the School of those who suspected its orthodoxy — an opposition which did much to attract young men of independent spirit.

In the summer of 1881 William Reed Huntington wrote to Dr. Wharton that the School was suffering "from the industrious circulation of reports of 'unsoundness' and 'rationalistic tendencies' " — reports which Huntington was contradicting and treating as libellous. Bishop Lawrence has said that the only bishops who sympathized with the School in the days of Dean Gray were Clark of Rhode Island, Whipple of Minnesota, and Potter of New York.

Dr. Allen, at the School's fortieth anniversary, spoke of the early rumors of its heresy: "We had hardly started when the suspicion was generated that we were in alliance with the movement for the Reformed Episcopal Church." This was because Bishop Cummins, who led that movement in 1872, had, three years before, lived at the School during a summer when everybody was away! "Then it was said that we were Unitarians," because of nearness to Harvard; and in the early eighties "reports were rife that we had departed generally from the Christian faith." When, in 1896, Allen reread the letter from Dr. Huntington, mentioned above, speaking of the reports of the School's unsoundness, he wrote: "This was in 1881. I think my *Continuity* was intended as an answer."

Although Dean Gray, as we have seen, was well aware of the advantages enjoyed by the School because of its proximity to Harvard and Harvard's friendly attitude, he was not blind to the disadvantages. Hence in 1887 he wrote to the Secretary of the College that while he realized that there was value "as an advertisement" in the University Catalogue's notice of the School, "yet there is the difficulty of frequent misapprehensions as to our relations to Harvard and possible injury to the School because of the strong prejudice against Harvard from a religious point of view." After that the notice ceased to appear.

In June, 1880, the Trustees endeavored to win over Bishop Paddock to a more favorable attitude to the School. They wrote to him that they were well aware of how much he could do to promote the School's prosperity and how detrimental to it was any "appearance of disaffection" on his part. Hence they invited him and the rest of the Board of Visitors to "the closest and most careful scrutiny of the School" and expressed a desire for their "friendly suggestions on all matters of interest to the institution."

To this the Visitors replied, in June, 1881, in a communication to the Trustees (drawn up by William Reed Huntington, then rector of All Saints', Worcester) on the School's daily worship, suggesting that it "might be made more interesting to the students if a more collegiate character were given to it," and if the Faculty attended more regularly. "To require the presence of each professor at least four times every week at one or other of the two daily services, would be to impose no hardship."

It was the custom at the time for each professor in turn to conduct the services for a week; those who were not conducting them seldom attended. Dr. Steenstra said he did not see how he could, considering the amount of teaching he was doing. (Ever since the opening of the School he had filled two chairs, giving all the instruction in Old Testament and New Testament, in Hebrew and in Greek.) Dr. Allen suspected that the Visitors were using the Chapel services as an entering wedge to get more control over the School. In our reply to them, he said, "Let us be cautious."

This was not enough for Steenstra, whose ire was up. "Let us," he rejoined, "be firm. I am not willing to be blown out of my course by the report of a body which, as a whole, has not visited the School. If we have to fight, this is as good a time as any. The Philistines will be on us again next year with another weapon."

Calmer counsels prevailed and the Faculty gave the Visitors' report "respectful consideration," deciding that they were "at liberty to follow their own judgment" in the matter, — which was to let the Chapel services continue as they were. Dr. Steenstra, however, despite his readiness to contest the issue with the Visitors, did actually begin to attend chapel when he was not leading it. The students, who knew nothing of the Visitors' report, said, "Steenie's got religion!"

The "Philistines" waited a year and a half and then delivered two more blows. One was a criticism of the teaching methods of the Faculty, the other a statement that the Chapel services were still unsatisfactory. The first was prepared by Dr. Samuel Eliot, Superintendent of Boston Schools, formerly President of Trinity College, Hartford.

This was the period when the Faculty were modulating over from the text book to the lecture, and Dr. Eliot and the other Visitors did not like it. In the lecture, they felt, the professor did the student's thinking for him. The Faculty, in a reply drawn up by Dr. Allen, agreed that daily recitations were admirable in preparatory school and useful perhaps in college, but the seminary, they said, was a professional school, whose students had already learned how to study and think for themselves and were "beyond the stage of dependence on the authority of a text-book." They pointed out that the lecture system was being adopted in all the better universities, but went on to say that a modified form of it was employed in the School. "I use a text book," said Allen, "which contains a condensed summary of the principal events. In the class room I examine the students on the portion assigned. I then lecture or comment upon the events in order to bring out their connection, to discover the causes which underlie them. I seek to induce the student to go beneath the surface and inquire for the real significance of a movement."

In the matter of chapel, the Visitors' strictures produced some effect. The Faculty said that they had decided henceforth to stress the morning service as the one at which both Faculty and students were all expected to be present, and that the Faculty would sit "in the sedilia, habited in surplices." Attendance at Evening Prayer would be optional. It would be conducted by the Faculty singly in turn.

Dean Gray, it seems, had been in sympathy with the Visitors' suggestions on this head. He wrote to William Reed Huntington, then on the point of going to Grace Church, New York: "It will please you to know that since your report about prayers, all my dreams (nearly) are realized — every morning *all* the professors attend in surplices! and we have choral service both A.M. and P.M."

In the fall of 1885 the Visitors came once more to the assault, this time, as Dr. Allen had suspected, to get control of the School. (William Reed Hntington was now no longer a Visitor, and Phillips Brooks, although he had been elected as one, had not yet attended a Visitors' meeting. The leading spirit appears to have been Dr. Samuel Eliot.) The Visitors complained that they had no real authority, and asked that some influence be given them "in the appointment of the dean and professors and the arrangement of studies," and that the Board of Trustees be enlarged "to comprise the bishop and a number of the clergy." "A theological school without theologians in its governing offices is," they said, "an anomaly."

Before replying, Robert C. Winthrop wrote to Dr. Wharton, then in Washington, for his advice, especially on the

proposal to put the bishop on the Board of Trustees. Wrote
Wharton: "I drew the charter and I not only knew Mr.
Reed's intentions in this matter, but I fully concurred in
his reasons. . . . The presence of a diocesan bishop in a
diocesan school has always been held mischievous. Bishop
McIlvaine always said this imperilled Gambier. Bishop
Meade to the end of his life declined to interfere in Alexandria Trustee meetings. Bishop Alonzo Potter, in framing
the constitution of the Philadelphia Seminary, put in two or
three other bishops, on the ground that a single diocesan
bishop would, by his presence, greatly embarrass the
board. The New York Seminary is preserved from this
difficulty by having *all* of the bishops members, who neu-
tralize each other by uniform disagreements.

"To have a *good* bishop a member as diocesan would
cripple your independence. You can consult him far more
efficiently if he is simply a Visitor. And a *bad* bishop, or an
able, despotic ecclesiastic, such as De Koven or Whitting-
ham! — you would either have to spend your time in fierce
antagonisms or make the School his puppet. Your only
course is to keep the bishop where he is."

With this emphatic support, Winthrop wrote the Trustees' reply. He pointed out that the organizational changes
suggested by the Visitors were beyond the power of the
Trustees under their charter; that it could hardly be desired
to have the bishop on *both* the Board of Trustees and the
Board of Visitors, and to transfer him from one to the other
did not commend itself to the judgment of the Trustees.
The founder, who undoubtedly sought the advice of such
leaders among the clergy as Dr. Vinton, Dr. Stone, Dr.
Wharton, Dr. (now Bishop) Huntington, and Bishop Eastburn, "came to the conclusion that his institution would be
managed with more harmony and more efficiency by a
small, self-perpetuating body of laymen." In answer to
their complaint of lack of power, the Visitors were re-

minded, perhaps with some irony, of the article in the
foundation instrument which declared that they "enjoy all
the rights and powers incident to the office of visitors of
eleemosynary institutions"! As for the suggested anomaly
that the School is a theological school without theologians
in its governing offices, "no such anomaly exists. . . . The
practical government of the School, in all its relations
to theological education, has been that of the Dean and
Faculty, all of whom are theologians of acknowledged
standing in the Church. . . . The main work of the Trustees hitherto has been to provide for the financial interests
of the institution — to take care of such funds as it possesses,
and to solicit, from time to time, the contributions necessary
for its support."

Shortly after this Dr. Samuel Eliot resigned and the Visitors subsided.

VII

CHANGES AND POLICIES

THE period of Dean Gray's administration was marked by changes in the Board of Trustees and additions to the Faculty. Between 1882 and 1884 all of the original Trustees, except Robert C. Winthrop, died or resigned. Among their successors were Judge Edmund H. Bennett, Robert Treat Paine, and Harcourt Amory, son of James S. Amory. Harcourt Amory served thirty-seven years, for all but one of which he was secretary of the Board. In the last year of Gray's deanship the number of Trustees was increased to seven. One of those chosen to fill out this number was Richard Henry Dana, who holds the record for length of service — forty-two years.

From the beginning of the School the Trustees had occasionally invited the Dean to attend their meetings. In 1883 they began with considerable regularity to do so, a custom they have continued to the present, so that the Dean has become essentially, though not legally, a member of the Board.[1]

As for the Faculty, Alexander H. Vinton, rector emeritus of Emmanuel Church, Boston, lectured in Theology — without salary — from 1877 till his death in 1881. In 1882 Dr. Wharton resigned. From January, 1882, till December, 1885, Elisha Mulford lectured in Theology and Apologetics. In the fall of 1882 Henry Sylvester Nash became an instruc-

---

[1] In 1927 Bishop Lawrence said: "I have sometimes wondered if the incorporation of the Dean in the body of the Trustees as chairman would not encourage firmer leadership."

tor. Late in 1883 he was elected Professor of the Literature and Interpretation of the New Testament, and William Lawrence Professor of Homiletics and Pastoral Care. In 1886 Max Kellner became Instructor in Hebrew, and in March, 1889, Assistant Professor. In June, 1889, a few months before Dean Gray's death, Edward Staples Drown was appointed Instructor in Theology.

We shall have occasion later to speak more fully of some of these teachers, but a word should be said here about Elisha Mulford, who, in his brief service, shed luster on the School.

Born in Montrose, Pennsylvania, in 1833, he graduated from Yale in 1855, studied at Union Seminary and Andover, was ordained in 1861, became rector at South Orange, New Jersey, but retired from the active ministry because of deafness in 1864. He devoted himself to study and writing at Lakeside, Pennsylvania, until 1880, when he came to live in Cambridge. When, in 1870, he published *The Nation*, he was, said Dr. Allen, "at once recognized as the ablest and profoundest student of political philosophy that the country had yet produced. . . . His book was preëminently a theological treatise, resting upon a religious conviction that the State was divine, that in the idea of the Nation God was present, embodying Himself as an indwelling force in human history." Just before coming to Cambridge he finished a volume of theology, which was published in 1881, and for which Dr. Allen suggested the title, *The Republic of God*.

"His appearance," said Allen, "arrested my attention before I knew who he was. He had a look of repose and of quiet assurance. His face disclosed the man who has a well-spring of inspiration within. It was a face capable of expressing the profoundest sadness, but for the most part there was written there a deep inward joy. In his manner of meeting you he impressed you as if he had long been waiting to know you; as if, would you only confide in him, you could tell him something of inestimable value. It was the same with all, especially with the students. He treated them with reverence as if there were in each an idea of God incorporated, which it was most important that he should know. It was not so much that he idealized as that he believed that the world and humanity had been already idealized through the Incarnation, thus giving him a ground for trusting his instincts. Hence the men whom he met were compelled to give him their best, and he always took them at their word.

"In theology he regarded Maurice as not only the greatest English theologian, but as surpassing the Germans on what had been accounted their chosen field."

It was his habit, said C. M. Addison, '82, who sat under him as a student, to come to class with a written lecture which he would proceed to read and which the men thought not too exciting. He would reach the end of it in about twenty minutes. This always seemed to surprise him and leave him at a loss as to what to do next. Then he would begin to talk, and he talked for the rest of the hour – so suggestively, so brilliantly, with such penetration that the men were spellbound.

Dr. Allen thought him "one of the greatest spiritual thinkers whom our age or country has produced." "The chief event with us here in Cambridge," wrote Allen in December, 1885, "is the death of Dr. Mulford. We shall miss him greatly. He usually spent two or three evenings each week in my study. He was the most interesting man I ever knew." Theodore T. Munger, the biographer of Horace Bushnell, wrote to Allen: "I think with you that Mulford was *great*, and with the most steadily intellectual play of mind that I have ever seen." "His talk," said Bishop Lawrence, "was like the running of smooth water, so quiet, so strong."

Whittier commemorated him thus:

Unnoted as the setting of a star
He passed; and sect and party scarcely knew
When from their midst a sage and seer withdrew
To fitter audience where the great dead are
In God's Republic of the heart and mind,
Leaving no purer, nobler soul behind!

It was in 1886 that the Faculty decided that the annual reports to the Trustees, written by the Dean in the name of the Faculty, and hitherto usually brief, should be fuller and written for publication.

That for 1888 described the life of the School:

"The day begins with breakfast at half-past seven, followed by Morning Prayer at half-past eight. At this service attendance is required of all, and the Faculty, present in the chancel, lead it in turn. On Wednesday and Friday the Litany is said, and at stated times the Holy Communion is administered. On other days the regular Order of Morning Prayer is followed, with one lesson; the chants, responses, and Psalter being sung. . . .

"The classes meet at ten and lectures last until one, except that on Monday [when there are afternoon classes] the morning is left free for study and that on Saturday there are no classes at all.[2] [There are] about fourteen hours of class work during the week. . . . In many institutions study is so arranged as to emphasize in each year some especial department. We prefer parallel progress in all departments. It would seem that continued attention to any topic for three years would lead to better results than confining it to one. . . . It is also in harmony with that continued study in all directions which should mark the clergyman subsequently.

"We have no roll call nor any system of marking [in

[2] Freedom from classes on Monday morning and on Saturday gave men time to prepare for Sunday work and to travel to and from it in days when there were no automobiles.

class]. . . . Our idea of instruction is that young men should be led and not dictated to or driven. We are aware that this is not the usual method, in our Church at any rate. The degree to which liberty of action and of thought is denied to Candidates is well known. . . .

"The afternoons are employed in study or in the library or in recreation. . . . At half-past five Evening Prayer is read by the professors in turn. On one day in the week this is followed by a sermon by members of the senior class in rotation, to which all remain. . . . After this service all meet for dinner in the refectory. . . . The management [of the refectory] is in the hands of a matron, under the supervision of Mr. Lawrence and a committee of one from each class, and in this way we have solved so far that difficult problem of all educational institutions." The refectory deficit "is now a little smaller" than last year. (Dean Gray was wont to speak of the refectory as the "refractory.")

"The School is known to be a place where men of many minds can learn to live in fraternal union . . . and where, while the instructors seek to impress their convictions, no student is less favored or respected because of honest adhesion to his own."

The report of 1889 added the following: "Professors and students meet upon the playground as well as in the class room. [It might have been noted that William Lawrence and E. S. Drown had issued a standing challenge to beat any two students at tennis]; the professors are as much at home in the students' rooms as are the students in the professors' houses. Thus lifelong friendships are formed. . . .

"Our own observation and the repeated testimony of the graduates assure us that with each year of residence there is a steady growth in spiritual life, self-discipline, and earnestness, and a deeper and more intelligent self-consecration."

In November, 1887, the St. John's Missionary Society was founded, later known simply as the St. John's Society, which proved then and since an additional bond of common interest for students and Faculty, for from its foundation Faculty and student body have been included in its membership.

In a note to one of the Trustees in December, 1883, Dean Gray said that the School was exercising, and was "destined still more largely to exercise an influence of great value as showing, to a degree unknown to our Church, the adjustment of the old faith to the new times." In an article on the School which he wrote in 1884 he said that its "aim has been to be independent of all schools of thought or parties, and to make the teaching as comprehensive as the Church itself." The annual reports from 1886 to 1889 enlarge on these themes:

"While adhering unflinchingly to the Church's standards, we must as firmly resist the claim of any party or transient school of thought to abridge the student's liberty. . . . Students must be encouraged to come to their own conclusions from the facts laid before them, and pace must be kept with the advance of the day in all branches of theological study. . . . This then is what the School stands for: candid, advanced, unpartizan, manly preparation for the ministry of Christ in this comprehensive Church. Nothing else is feasible in the presence of a great university, where men have learned to think for themselves."

"Our system of training must be in consistent and thorough accord with the spirit of our Church. That spirit is Catholicity in its true sense. . . . Again it is clearly demanded that our methods be modern in a place where the art of instruction has reached so high a development. . . . The studies required must be pursued in a mature way, books prepared for scholars are to be used, and no issue is to be evaded."

"The ministry will not be strengthened by pressing half-educated men into Holy Orders. Whatever may be felt to be the necessity in other parts of the country, our duty here is plain: to educate young men, not merely to pass the canonical examinations and to meet the average requirements of the Church, but to give to the Church men who will be leaders of thought and action, and will earn for her a high regard in our communities of educated people. . . .

"In our methods of study we do not yield but rather insist upon large liberty of thought, wide as well as thorough reading, and the frank expression of opinion. . . . The instructor's work is not the hearing of lessons so much as the inspiring and guiding the students to thought and research."

Bishop Lawrence, recently looking back on these reports, said, "We to-day have no conception of the revolutionary note here struck." While "the search for truth had become the touchstone of reality" in education generally, "the schools of theology were pursuing the old method of text book instruction, of conforming to authority and accepting implicitly what the professors taught their pupils." Hence the publication of the aims and methods of study at Cambridge "was a challenge to every theological school and to the prevailing temper of the Church. It set this School to the fore."

A secular newspaper, *The Cambridge Tribune*, commented editorially on Dean Gray's report for 1887: "It is said that the Episcopal Church is growing rapidly in America, and if the modes of thought and of instruction that are marked out in this report are characteristic of the body as a whole, the faster it grows the better."

While the method and spirit of the teaching at the School had been changing, as well as the content of some of the courses, the subjects taught and the time allotted to them remained much the same. This was to be expected in the light of canonical requirements. However, in Dean Gray's first year there was a course of lectures given at the School on the Relations of Science and Religion by Professor John

McCrady, Professor of Zoölogy at Harvard; in 1878 an "Introduction to the Study of Ethnic Religions" became a regular part of Dr. Allen's Senior Church History and remained so till 1890; in 1887 the Dean and Faculty said the School needed a chair in the relation of Christianity "to questions connected with social science and physical and metaphysical inquiry"; in 1885 Professor Steenstra acknowledged that for most men the study of Hebrew was a waste of time; and in 1888, in response to a petition from the students, Hebrew was no longer required after the middle year. This was the first serious dent in the prescribed curriculum.

In the last report written by Dean Gray, that of 1888, the School's conception of the ministry is thus set forth: the minister must be "above all devoted to Christ"; he "must be loyal to the Church"; he "must be manly, trusted for his integrity as well as respected for his sagacity"; he must be "ready to recognize labor for God wherever real," and he "must be thoroughly in sympathy with this land and this people." "We minister to a people who have a healthy contempt for all affectation, yet strangeness of speech and demeanor and dress appear to be growing rapidly in our Church. . . . In measure as un-American elements are introduced, in that measure is this Church afflicted by her sons. If it is to be the American Church it must have a ministry more truly and thoroughly American than that of any competitors for that position. Such is the kind of men we seek to send into the ministry, and we feel encouraged by the results obtained."

The year before, it had been pointed out that the Alumni were serving in thirty-four dioceses and missionary districts. "They are of no one exclusive stripe, but are associated with all the different schools of thought in our Church, carrying into all a manly independence of party trammels and a wide and tolerant sympathy."

In the report for 1889, the last of Dean Gray's administration, but penned by Professor Lawrence, it was said that the final test of the School lay in the spirit and lives of the Alumni. "Tried by this test, the School has every cause for congratulation. That they are loyal to the Saviour and the Church is a matter of course; that they are able ministers of the New Testament and have positions of wide usefulness and heavy responsibility in all parts of the land and in foreign fields is what we who have known them would expect. But that they should turn back to the School with loving devotion and repeated expressions of thankfulness for their residence here, is a cause for deep gratitude."

Arthur Rogers, '89, several years after his graduation, expressed the feeling of the men of this era for the School: "There are certain places which twine themselves about one's heart-strings, and grow dearer and dearer as the years go by. Surely Cambridge is such a place. I remember well the dismal homesickness of my first two days there, and the happiness of all the time that followed. There was not a classroom in which there was not inspiration."

Sherrard Billings, '84, speaking of the School in behalf of the older alumni in 1912, said: "It has grown singularly deep into the affections of us all, very singularly deep."

The Alumni had met at the School annually at Commencement time since 1874, and in 1889 they voted to make the Mid-Winter Alumni Quiet Day, which had been held informally for some years, a regular institution.

In June, 1888, Professor Lawrence was made Vice-Dean, at the request of Dean Gray. The Dean, although only fifty years old and of apparently robust constitution, was stricken with Bright's disease. On return from a rest in Bermuda in the spring of 1889, he was taken suddenly ill while lecturing at Wellesley College and "without any premonition blindness came upon him." He made a partial recovery and planned to spend the year 1889–90 in Europe, but in August, 1889, he died at Sharon, New York.

He had, said the Trustees, won the confidence of everyone connected with the School "by the kindness of his heart, the wisdom of his counsels, and his eminent executive ability."

VIII

DEAN LAWRENCE

WILLIAM LAWRENCE'S election to the deanship in September, 1889, was a foregone conclusion, for he had been called as professor on the understanding that he would succeed Dean Gray. He was thirty-nine years old, the son of Amos A. Lawrence, late Trustee, Treasurer, and benefactor of the School. He had been born on May 30, 1850, but, as he often reminded us, not on Memorial Day. He was eighteen when that day was first observed. He graduated from Harvard in 1871, read history for a year as a graduate student, was drawn to the ministry by the example of Phillips Brooks, studied theology first at Andover, then in Philadelphia, and finally, for the Easter term of 1875, in Cambridge. He received his B.D. from the School that year. He then became assistant to the Rev. George Packard at Grace Church, Lawrence, Massachusetts. A year later, on Dr. Packard's death, he was chosen rector.

Dean Gray appears to have been the first to suggest him as a possible professor, but no sooner was the suggestion made than it received unanimous approval. As Dr. Allen said at the time, his character and his work at Lawrence commanded "universal respect throughout the diocese." He began teaching in Cambridge in January, 1884. In addition to his teaching he acted as pastor to the Harvard students who attended St. John's Chapel, relieved the Dean of half the Sunday preaching, and, in the last two years of the Dean's life, took over many of his administrative duties.

There is varying witness as to his teaching ability. He was

not, in the opinion of Dr. Drown, a good teacher; he lacked assurance and apologized too much. Dean Washburn, whose student days came five years after Drown's, thought Lawrence's teaching admirable, and was impressed by his use of religious biography. According to Lawrence's own testimony he insisted on simplicity and naturalness in preaching and the avoidance, as of poison, of a conventional pulpit manner and a pulpit language. "Again and again," he said, "I have compelled men to rewrite their sermons, translating every abstract, philosophical, theological, trite, and conventional word and phrase into language which the average man and woman understands."

On becoming Dean he did not move into the deanery. He had, in 1887, purchased the Hastings estate (known to recent graduates as Dr. Richard Cabot's house) on Brattle Street, between the School and the Longfellow House. He continued to live there. One day a visitor inquired for him at his home. "He's not here," said one of his small daughters, "he's over at the Illogical School."

The deanery was rented to Professor George Herbert Palmer of Harvard, who, with his distinguished wife, Alice Freeman Palmer, occupied it during Lawrence's deanship.

Lawrence was Dean for only four years, but those years were a flowering period for the School. It goes without saying that he was superbly fitted for the deanship. His Christian integrity, his parochial and academic experience, his sanity, balance, and business ability, his social and family connections, his wealth and the generosity with which he used it, his skill in opening the pocket books of others — all these qualities contributed signally to the welfare of the School. But he was also fortunate in the time at which he acceded to office. Dean Gray had left the School with a growing reputation, a physical equipment almost perfect for its size, an increasing student body, and an able and enthusiastic faculty in which youth predominated.

When Lawrence became Dean, Steenstra, the senior

professor, was only fifty-six, Allen was forty-eight, Nash thirty-five, Kellner and Drown both twenty-eight. Their average age was thirty-nine, which was exactly Lawrence's age. There have been few if any periods in the School's life in which the Faculty exhibited at once so much ability, so much promise, and so much youth.

As Bishop Clark of Rhode Island said in his sermon at the School's Commencement in 1891: "During the last few years there has been a great advance in the training for the ministry. . . . Professorships are no longer made to serve as a resort and resting-place for retired invalids."

Phillips Brooks had always been a friend of the School, but in its early years had judged other seminaries better. In 1872 he had advised Lawrence to take at least part of his theological course at Andover. In 1891 he told C. L. Slattery, then a student at Harvard, that the School was "beyond all doubt the best."

Bishop Doane of Albany, who might have been supposed to think otherwise, told his Convention in 1890 that he had visited Cambridge and come away with "a most pleasant impression of the work done in the School, and of great satisfaction in the wisdom and courage of those who planted under the shadow of Harvard University an institution of sound religious teaching."

Bishop Clark, in his address to the Rhode Island Convention of 1892, said, "This seminary is in a thriving condition. The attractiveness of the location, the singular beauty of the buildings, the literary standing of the School, the thoroughness of instruction, the clear apprehension on the part of the teachers of the modes of thought peculiar to the age, all combine to give this institution a high and honorable rank, and serve to account for the enthusiastic love with which the Alumni regard it."

Phillips Brooks, who was consecrated Bishop of Massachusetts in October, 1891, took occasion, in his first and

only Convention address, the next year, publicly to commend the School: "We may well be specially and profoundly thankful that we have in our great seminary at
Cambridge a home and nursery of faith and learning, . . .
which no School of our Church has ever surpassed. Full
of deep sympathy with present thought; quick with the
spirit of inquiry; eager to train its men to think and reason;
equipped with teaching power of the highest order; believing in the ever-increasing manifestation of the truth of God;
anxious to blend the most earnest piety with the most active
intelligence, and so to cultivate a deep, enthusiastic, reasonable faith, the Cambridge School stands very high among
the powers which bid us hope great things."

Said Dean Lawrence in his annual report in June, 1891:
"The increasing number of letters coming from all parts of
the country, asking for our graduates, is one of the most
hopeful features of our work."

A secular newspaper, commenting on the School's
twenty-fifth anniversary, remarked that there had been a
day when bishops refused to send their candidates to Cambridge, "but now it is the one place where every young man
in the Episcopal Church who amounts to anything feels that
he must go."

Perhaps the most revealing tribute to the School was that
of Franklin Spencer Spalding (later Bishop of Utah). He
was a student at the General Seminary from 1888 to 1891.
His father, the Bishop of Colorado, peremptorily forbade
his candidates to study at Cambridge, and Franklin Spencer
knew little about the School until, in January, 1890, he attended a missionary convention in Cambridge. After his
return to New York he wrote: "The fellowship between
Faculty and students at Cambridge is wonderful. Silver took
me into Professor Kellner's room and I talked to him about
Higher Criticism for two hours. He thinks Moses wrote no
more than the Decalogue, and that Leviticus is the latest

book of the Five, and that the existence of the Tabernacle is very doubtful. He also thinks that Assyrian inscriptions are more reliable for determining chronology than the Bible, with which they often disagree; and yet he spoke with suspicion of the 'Rationalists.' We hear absolutely nothing of this here, and when we ask questions the answer shows that the professor is as poorly read on the subject as we are. I don't wonder Cambridge students are fond of their seminary."

In 1883, the Visitors had criticized adversely the teaching methods of the School. In 1893, they were "impressed with the increased numbers, and the general appearance of maturity and interest in all the classes, as well as the thoroughness and ability manifested by the professors."

It was of the School's teaching staff at this time that Howard Chandler Robbins once wrote: "No other seminary in the Episcopal Church, or perhaps in the entire Anglican Communion, could boast a faculty of men of greater ability or more entirely devoted to the search for truth."

The number of students enrolled during the four years of Lawrence's deanship was forty-three, forty-seven, forty-five, and forty-two. The slight drop in the latter years was due to a stiffening of entrance requirements. In 1892 an A.B. was required for admission to regular standing, and two years of college work for admission as a special student. In that year the Dean reported to the Trustees that the proportion of men in the School who had a college degree was "greater than that in any Harvard Professional School — Law, Medicine, or Divinity, and greater than that in any theological school of our Church."

It was in this period that the social concern of the students began to be awakened, chiefly by Professor Nash. In the fall of 1892 he gathered some dozen students round him for the weekly study of the relation of the Church to social problems. They called themselves "My Neighbor Club." The group continued a thriving existence, eventually doubling its membership, until 1905, when it merged with and brought its interests into the reorganized St. John's Society.

"My first aim [as Dean]," said Lawrence, "was to unite in even closer sympathy than before the teachers and students as one family. . . . I stayed 'on the job,' believing as I do that the public character of an educational institution is not made by the speeches of its deans or president moving about the country, but by the graduates. . . . The presence of the Dean in chapel morning and evening, the fact that he is at the service of the students every day of the week, and his personal leadership in the routine are vital to the welfare of a school."

He was open to advice from the students, and at the suggestion of Atkinson, '93, and Slattery, '94, instituted a weekly Chapel address by a member of the Faculty, and "at Lent and some other seasons a late compline conducted by the students."

He was also ready to approve of changes in the time honored curriculum. In 1890 the students petitioned for a readjustment of the course of study, so that they would not have to pursue so many subjects at one time. Steenstra and Allen, who were appointed to consider the matter, reported "insuperable difficulties" in arranging a curriculum which would avoid this, but they did suggest certain changes, so that "speaking roughly the main stress will be laid on the Scriptures in the junior year, on History in the middle year, and on Systematic and Practical Theology in the senior year."

A more significant change was the introduction, on a small scale, of the elective system. We recall how, under Dean Gray in 1888, Hebrew was no longer required in the senior year. Old Testament study in English was substituted for those who did not continue Hebrew. Three years later required Hebrew in the middle year was abandoned and the time given to it in the junior year reduced by a fourth. The freed time was to be used for directed reading in other fields. Thus the "reading course," which we are apt to regard as of recent origin, was introduced as early as 1891. The next year specific elective courses were also offered: Pauline Ethics, Maurice's Theology, Psalms, and Job. In 1893 New England Religious Thought and Modern Movements in the Anglican Church were added.

To an editorial in *The Churchman* in 1891, complaining that our seminaries made no adequate provision for instruction in Christian Ethics, Dean Lawrence replied: "This School makes that study the basis of its three year course. Our approach to Apologetics and Theology is from the ethical standpoint, and on ethical principles our theological study is built."

The Catalogue of 1889–90 was the last to mention either public examinations or, for candidates for the B.D., "an especial examination covering the studies of the whole course." After that all men who had entered with a college degree and had "sustained a rank satisfactory to the Faculty," and presented an acceptable thesis were to receive the B.D. The certificate was retained for those who fell short of these requirements.

In 1890 the School was able to offer its first scholarships — two of $150 each, as the result of a bequest of $6,000 from Mrs. James B. Dow.

The death of Dean Gray had left the School without a professor of Systematic Divinity. E. S. Drown, '89, was appointed, immediately on graduation, instructor in this field, but was felt to be too young to do all the teaching in it. Professor Nash took some of it, in addition to his New Testament work, and visiting lecturers were secured for short courses. This arrangement continued for three years, during which Bishop Frederic Dan Huntington, The Rev.

William Reed Huntington, Stewart Means, '76, and the Rt. Rev. William Alexander, Lord Bishop of Derry and Raphoe, were among the visiting lecturers. At the end of that time Trustees, Faculty, and students had come to the conclusion that E. S. Drown was a better teacher of theology than any of these stars. He was, accordingly, elected Assistant Professor in 1892, and took over all the courses.

As early as 1873 Dean Stone had asked the Trustees to appoint a teacher of reading and elocution. Dean Gray, who spoke of the subject as "sacred oratory," repeated the request, but it was not until the last year of his deanship that the Trustees felt able to employ a temporary part-time man in this field. Dean Lawrence had received benefit from private voice lessons while in parish work and was convinced that the value of voice instruction in the School could not be overemphasized. As he said, "The bad reading, imperfect enunciation, uncultivated voices, and unfortunate manner of many of our clergy often make our beautiful service a dismal performance." In 1890 he secured John J. Hayes, Instructor in Elocution at Harvard, as a part-time teacher at the School. Mr. Hayes continued in this position for nine years.

In 1892 the School, for the first time, engaged a librarian, Miss Edith D. Fuller, who served for thirty-three years, until her retirement in 1924.[1] Besides her efficient and devoted management of the library, she is remembered for a classic remark: one day when the children of Dean Lawrence's successor, Dean Hodges, were making an unholy racket just outside the library, she was heard to mutter, as she paced wrathfully up and down beside the window near-

---

[1] She was succeeded by her assistant, Miss Helen D. Beals, in 1924. Miss Grace A. Littell, the present librarian, was called in 1926. Since then she has recatalogued the entire library according to the system devised especially for theological libraries by Union Seminary. The library contains about 37,000 volumes.

est them, "This makes you believe in the celibacy of the clergy."

The period of Lawrence's deanship was marked by an expansion in physical equipment. The Chapel congregation added the robing room to the Chapel as a memorial to Dean Gray. Thanks to a legacy from Robert Means Mason and a gift from his daughters, the Chapel organ was rebuilt and moved from the gallery to its present position, and the front pews, which faced the chancel, without a central aisle, were replaced by the choir stalls we now have. At the Dean's suggestion, the family of John Appleton Burnham added matron's and servants' quarters and store rooms to the refectory. A modern bathroom and hot water system was installed in Lawrence Hall by the Lawrence family — which included the Dean. And finally the Dean suggested to the Trustees that there was no more fitting way to celebrate the twenty-fifth anniversary of the School than by building a new dormitory and naming it after their President, the only living member of the original board, Robert C. Winthrop. The cost would be $75,000. At the time he made this staggering suggestion he hastened to add that during the preceding fortnight he had mentioned it to half a dozen friends and relatives of Mr. Winthrop and had secured subscriptions for $46,000, which included his own gift of the land, valued at $10,000, on which the dormitory was to stand. It was completed in 1893 and its entire cost paid.

In addition to this, almost $10,000 a year for current expenses were contributed by friends of the School during Lawrence's administration.

The School was stunned when, on January 23, 1893, it heard that Phillips Brooks was dead. From the time of his coming to Boston he had been a frequent visitor to the School. On becoming Bishop he had come to see each of his candidates individually. "Regardless of churchmanship," said C. L. Slattery, "the men were all his ardent dis-

ciples." When news of his death came "we could not believe it. We wandered aimlessly from room to room to ask
each other how it could be." "To young men who had felt
that for once they had seen a man of the stamp of Plato or
Dante — one of the few greatest souls of all time — it seemed
as if the props of the world had fallen away."

Next morning in chapel Dean Lawrence chose the Beati-
tudes for the Lesson, and when he came to "Blessed are ye,
when men shall revile you, and persecute you," the memory of the unjust accusations against Brooks at the time of
his election as bishop, swept over him and, as he said, "for
the first and only time in a service I broke down completely." Nash stepped forward and continued.

On May 4 Lawrence was elected Brooks' successor, the
first alumnus of the School to be chosen as a bishop. Five
days later he resigned as Dean, to take effect at the coming
Commencement.

In his last report to the Trustees, he spoke of the large
opportunity which lay before the School and of its needs.
A modern theological school, he said dare not be a monastic
institution. It must be in touch with the intellectual life and
the social problems of the time, yet it must also afford the
possibility of retirement from them. This School, he said,
is ideally placed to meet these conditions. "Situated in the
midst of the most peculiarly university town in the country,
we are at the same time in close touch with a community of
over a million people, with all the modern problems before
us; while in our quiet quadrangle and Chapel, our independent organization and our family life, we have the possible
retirement of the mystic." "No School in the country has
a possible future equal to this."

To meet this future adequately the School, he maintained,
ought to have a professor of Social Ethics, another of Comparative Religion, another of Liturgics and Canon Law, a
second professor in the New Testament Department, and

one of Homiletics and Pastoral Care, separate from the deanship. It ought to have a publication foundation, and funds for graduate fellowships, and a pastor for Episcopal college students.

It will doubtless be said, he concluded, that this is over ambitious, but "if a Boston churchman had been told thirty years ago that there would be in Cambridge, the center of Unitarianism, a thriving School of our Church, with a beautiful plant of buildings worth several hundred thousands of dollars, and friends who give annually to its support ten thousand dollars, he would have refused to believe it."

He also took occasion to speak of the devotional life of the School. An impression, he said, sometimes gets abroad "that theological seminaries dry up the foundations of religious enthusiasm and that schools which favor intellectual life and modern critical methods are peculiarly barren in their culture of personal religion. . . . This is not true of the Cambridge School. And we confidently summon as witnesses the whole body of alumni. . . . They assure us that their spiritual life was quickened here. They turn to this place in grateful remembrance of its spiritual gifts to them. And in preparation for Lent they come back each year for mutual converse and prayer."

"There has seemed to me," he said in his letter of resignation to the Trustees, "no position in the Church so full of happy and useful opportunities as this which I now resign. . . . I pray God that his spirit may dwell in this place from generation to generation."

He continued to live in his house beside the School till 1910, and, until his death at the age of ninety-one in 1941, remained the School's wisest counsellor, its most effective helper, and its best friend.

IX

STEENSTRA AND ALLEN

GRANTED the generosity of Benjamin Tyler Reed and the other early benefactors, granted the organizing and guiding wisdom of Wharton, Stone, Gray, and Lawrence, what really made the School for the first forty years of its life was the teaching of Steenstra and Allen. Both began to teach at the opening of the School; both continued on with but little diminution of vigor through the first half of the deanship of Lawrence's successor, George Hodges. But since they were unquestionably at their prime in the days of Dean Lawrence it may be well to consider them here.

Peter Henry Steenstra or, as he was affectionately called, "Steenie," was born in Holland, at Donjum near Franeker in Friesland, in 1833. He was brought to this country by his parents at the age of eleven and raised in St. Louis among the straightest sect of the Baptists. His father died when he was twelve, his mother when he was sixteen. He worked in a printing office for some years before entering Rochester University, New York. When his St. Louis pastor was made head of the new Shurtleff College in Illinois, he left Rochester for Shurtleff, whence he graduated in 1858. He was pastor of the Stoughton Street Baptist Church in Dorchester, Massachusetts, for nearly four years, until 1864, when he was ordained by Bishop Eastburn and became rector of Grace Church, Newton. There he began the translation of Lange's Commentary on Judges and Ruth, which he published later. From Newton he was called to the School.

After serving the School for forty years, he retired at the age of seventy-four in 1907. He died in 1911. As Dean Hodges said at the time of Steenstra's retirement, he had become so much a part of the School's life that the Alumni felt he was essential to its existence. "When [as students] they came they found him; and when, after graduation, they came back, there he was to bid them welcome. When they thought of the School they thought of him. . . . The School has been his life to a degree unusual among teachers."

He was one of the first Biblical scholars in this country to see and to lead his students to see the significance of the critical and historical study of the Bible, begun by the German scholars of his and a previous generation. But his conclusions were not reached easily or without pain. He was a conservative by nature and he had been brought up with the traditional view of the Bible. Said Allen: "I met Steenstra in 1867. . . . He was one of the most conservative men that I ever knew. It was like pulling teeth, every step that he took. You have hardly any conception of what the steps were we were taking. In those early days we were discussing very painfully whether or not the world was actually made in the year four thousand and four and in the spring of the year; whether the evening and the morning of March 25 were the first day. And we were very much exercised over the question whether the deluge was partial or complete."

At the time of his retirement Steenstra called attention to the transition in theological thought during his years of teaching, "a transition the greatness of which," he said, "I believe few of us yet understand. The mediation of that transition, within the limits of this School, it was both my task and my privilege to conduct. It was an event of which I think few theological teachers have experience. When I came here I was under the still strong influence of the old theory about the Bible — that God had revealed himself in a book and that the book had been written by infallibly inspired men. I had difficulties with these conceptions from the time that I was twenty years old. Even almighty power cannot inspire a man infallibly unless he converts the man into a mere typewriting machine.

"For twenty years I was turning over all that I could lay hands on of what had been written on the origin of the Pentateuch, for there the battle began. Fought out there, it was fought out for the Bible as a whole. . . . It was not until Wellhausen published his epoch-making book that we really got light on the subject. . . . That was the liberating book. The moment I read it I had the solution of my difficulties."

Said C. L. Slattery, '94, in his biography of his friend Edward Lincoln Atkinson, '93, "Dr. Steenstra, though the senior professor, was reading every new book to get the last word for his department. Atkinson, with all others, felt the rugged honesty and power of this profound student, and learned not only Old Testament Interpretation, but a great lesson in sincerity."

Steenstra, said Bishop Lawrence, never stopped growing. And to illustrate this he used to tell of the occasion when, after a Matriculation Service, he noticed Steenstra starting toward his home. "Aren't you coming to the Matriculation dinner?" asked Lawrence. "No," said Steenstra, "I have to prepare my lecture for to-morrow." "Why not use last year's?" queried Lawrence. "I can't," was the reply, "I no longer believe it."

"In these last weeks of his professorship," said Dean Hodges in 1907, "Steenstra is still reading the newest books." And speaking of his services in imparting to his students the contributions of German Biblical scholars, the Dean added: "A certain natural piety and evangelical faith kept him from following these writers into conclusions which his religious instincts refused, but he has never been 'nervously ortho-dox,' that is, he has never been in fear lest something should happen to the truth. He has been in no more distress as to the effect of the critics on the Bible than as to the effect of the astronomers on the stars.

"He is a teacher in whom faith and fearlessness meet. . . . He has a fine impatience of superficial work, of pleasant fallacies, of conclusions which cost nothing, and of opinions whose chief merit is that for the moment they are 'safe.' He believes that nothing is permanently safe except the everlasting and invincible truth."

Referring to his early training as a Baptist, the Dean went on to say, "He has not only the clearness of conviction which belongs so often to those who have read themselves into the Church, but — what is more unusual — he brought with him a profound respect for the piety and the learning of the brethren among whom he had been brought up. He was able to interpret to his pupils, out of his own experience, the significance of those forms of Protestantism which many Churchmen fail to understand. He had none of the ecclesiastical provincialism which imagines that all the truth is contained within the narrow limits of one's own opinion."

H. S. Nash, '81, first his student, then his assistant, said of him: "I have been in Dr. Steenstra's intellectual companionship for nearly thirty years. More than any other mind I have personally known, his mind impresses me as a rare union of clearness, candor, and restraint. It has always taken time for the students to learn to appreciate him. . . . The real students in the School have felt in him an intelligence so much larger than any opinion or set of opinions that Truth in her cleansing and creating power has become for them a real presence."

Steenstra published little. Beside the commentaries already mentioned, there was a volume of theology, *The Being of God as Trinity and Unity*, 1891, and chapters on Hebrew History and Literature in Wright's *History of All Nations*, 1905. Dr. Drown used to say that Steenstra found Biblical learning developing so rapidly that by the time he had anything ready for publication it was already out of date.

He was a forthright person and did not mince his words. When Augustine Heard Amory, '80, gave some lectures at the School in 1890, Steenstra, because of deafness, read them in manuscript. He wrote to Amory in enthusiastic commendation, but added: "There is one point against which I flatly and ferociously demur, viz. the statement that the ideal choir is the boy and man choir. That to me is as heretical and irrational as it would be to say that the ideal Paradise would be one that had no Eve in it. . . . Who but the arch-enemy of mankind would say to women, Go on the stage and celebrate secular themes, but keep out of the Church?" A train of thought was started by something Amory said about the term *Rector*. "I have often growled at it," said Steenstra, "but am now inclined to hold on to it for dear life as a strong defense against over-strained notions of episcopal authority. It implies the independence of the parish and its chosen head against episcopal domination. . . . The bishop may be *pastor pastorum*, but he is not *rector rectorum*."

Steenstra was a bluff, bearded figure, somewhat choleric, and increasingly deaf as the years went by. To the students he was increasingly diverting. A photograph of the Commencement procession crossing the School grounds in 1894 shows him vested in surplice and straw hat; in winter he invariably wore his galoshes while leading worship in chapel; he frequently made blunders in the service, such as turning over two pages of the Psalms at once and, owing to his deafness, not noticing the difference between the responses of the congregation and the text he was reading. On one occasion he began Morning Prayer by characteristically announcing the wrong hymn. Then, after the General Confession and Absolution, went on, not to the Lord's Prayer but to the second Absolution, at that time printed as an alternative immediately after the first. The Dean, beside him, roared, "Our Father," so loudly in his ear that he became aware that he was being corrected. This peeved him, so when he came, in a moment, to announce the Psalter, he said, "Psalm ninety-two, to the best of my knowledge and belief."

He occasionally perpetrated spoonerisms. Once when he came to the words in the Psalter: "Their eyes swell with fatness," he read, "Their eyes fell with swatness." He noticed the mistake and tried again, but again he read, "Their eyes fell with swatness." He shrugged his shoulders and went on.

He felt that the ideal method of education was that which stimulated but did not compel the student to work. Hence he did not listen with enthusiasm to a report on requirements for the degree prepared by the youthful H. S. Nash and E. S. Drown in 1889. Recognizing that although the spirit be willing, the flesh, even in theological students, may be weak, Nash and Drown recommended that the Faculty put a bit more pressure on the students or, as they phrased it, "quicken the pace." This roused the wrath of Steenstra. He restrained himself at the time but the fire smouldered. At the Commencement dinner it burst forth. "You'll be glad to hear," he boomed at the gathered Alumni, "that we're quickening the pace — quickening the pace so much that some men who have been here two years propose to take their third in Germany; if we keep on quickening the pace a man can get all he needs here in one year and go to Germany after that; if we only quicken the pace sufficiently, in a short time students will come to Cambridge and take one look at the Faculty and then go to Germany!"

His examinations were unique. In Dean Hodges' Journal occurs this entry: "Steenstra examines the seniors, 1902, by having them draw lots. Two lots are marked 'IT,' and the men drawing them are each asked a question, and then the whole class is marked B!"

One day when J. W. Suter, '85, returning to the School as an alumnus, called on Steenstra, he found him reading with interest an alluring invitation to invest in Mexican rubber. Suter took the prospectus, said he would consult his friends in State Street about it, and later wrote to the Professor that it was a swindle. In reply he received a post card on which was written simply, "Psalm 73: 2,3," over Steenstra's initials. On consulting the Authorized Version Suter found: "As for me, my steps had well nigh slipped, for I was envious at the foolish, when I saw the prosperity of the wicked."

At the time of Steenstra's retirement, H. B. Washburn, '94, said of him, "Simple as a child, honest as the daylight, scornful of cant and hypocrisy, a passionate devotee of the truth, he started out forty years ago almost single handed and fought hard for the freedom of the Old Testament, and he has lived to see the victory."

H. S. Nash, a year after Steenstra's death, said: "Just now Biblical Criticism is in fashion in all the seminaries of our Church; but there was a time, and it lasted twenty or twenty-five years, when there was only one school in this Church of ours that was doing criticism — only one, and you owe it to Steenstra."

Steenstra was thirty-four when he was called to the School. Allen was twenty-six. Steenstra taught for forty years, Allen for forty-one, until his death in 1908.

Alexander Viets Griswold Allen was born in 1841 in Otis, Massachusetts, where his father was rector of the church. He was named for and baptized by the Bishop. His boyhood was spent in Nantucket, Massachusetts, and Guilford, Vermont, where his father held cures. In 1862 he was graduated from Kenyon College where, as we have seen, he had come under the spell of Francis Wharton. He stayed on in Gambier for two years studying theology at Bexley Hall, and then, at the suggestion of Wharton, who had meanwhile come to Brookline, he transferred to the Seminary at Andover and worked as a student assistant to the Rev. George Packard, rector of Grace Church, Lawrence. In this capacity he started St. John's Mission. After graduation and ordination in 1865, he stayed for a year's graduate study at Andover, continuing in charge of St. John's. This became a parish in 1866 with Allen as rector. From there he was called to the School.

Professor Park of Andover recommended him highly, saying, "He could fill the chair of Hebrew Literature or Greek Exegesis or Ecclesiastical History with credit to himself and with usefulness to any theological seminary." He was called to teach Ecclesiastical History, but as Dean Gray was wont to say, there was no need of chairs in any other subject, for Allen taught them all.

Said Allen of himself, "I am always moving underground, beneath institutions and customs and formulas of thought, and trying to get at some deeper meaning." "To study history is to bring one near to the process of God, that is, the study of it upon a large scale, which takes in great reaches of events. 'The undevout astronomer is mad.' The same might be said of the undevout historian." Said C. L. Slattery, '94, the result of his teaching was "to make men feel how tight a hold God has upon human affairs."

From the first he aroused the enthusiasm of his students. E. L. Stoddard, '71, wrote: "All deficiencies of this newly created and necessarily incomplete seminary were made up for one hundred fold by Prof. A. V. G. Allen. His interpretation of the development of the Church, his revelation of what our Church really meant and stood for, why it could afford to be comprehensive in its theology and its practice, filled me with admiration then and have been sources of inspiration for over fifty years. God be thanked that I came under a man like Allen."

Said Stewart Means, '76, writing for the *Dictionary of American Biography*, "He was a great teacher."

"When, in the list of things for which I bless God, I think of my teachers," said H. S. Nash, '81, "I think of his name above all. . . . In his class room history became a real presence. Up out of the dead, dull, monotonous past stepped great distinguished things into life. . . . He had the art of doing for us what Augustine said the first reading of Plato did for him: He kindled in me an almost incredible flame of desire to know."

E. S. Drown, '89, repeatedly said that although he had studied with Palmer and Royce and Harnack, no one of them, as a teacher, had come anywhere near Allen.

When C. L. Slattery, '94, was an undergraduate at Harvard he first heard Allen at a public lecture. "On that night," said Slattery, "I recognized that he was more of a humanist than any man I had known. Distinguished masters had taught me Greek and Latin and English and philosophy, but none of them seemed to have quite this same human sympathy for the genius of the past. . . . I awaited the day when I might call myself his pupil. When that day came I found him more than a humanist. He was revealed as a prophet." And speaking for himself and his classmates in the Theological School, Slattery added, "We all averred, though we might formerly have sat under James or Norton or Shaler, that we had never known such a teacher." "Sometimes [after his lecture] we went to our rooms as if we had been present at some searching and inspiring service. Our hearts had been lifted up."

In his Life of E. L. Atkinson, '93, Slattery wrote: "Atkinson felt that Dr. Allen was the most inspiring teacher he had ever known. Men went to his lecture-room with the facts they had read; they came away with the meaning of the facts; and day by day they felt the majesty of God's purpose working itself out with irresistible strength in human history. Not the least delightful aspects of Dr. Allen's course were the informal Tuesday evening seminars where he met the class in the reading room of Lawrence Hall. Three men ordinarily read papers, to which the master gave such attention as was at once encouraging and humiliating. He frequently interrupted the reader with illuminating and appreciative comment. . . . Men who perhaps had never known what scholarship was, learned it at last in Dr. Allen's seminars."

"He treated his students," said Slattery, "as if they were his equals. He never talked down to them." They "were always his first thought. No glitter of wider fame ever blinded his eyes to his real task."

For several years Allen's salary was only $1400 a year and a house. The Trustees realized that this was inadequate, but felt unable to pledge themselves to a permanent increase. They did, however, make occasional extra grants. In 1881 there was one of $500. On receipt of it Allen wrote to Amos A. Lawrence: "I wish to acknowledge with many thanks the check for $500. . . . I have two aims in life, one is to study the history of the Christian Church and teach it effectively to theological students, and the other is to keep out of debt. The accomplishment of the latter aim helps the former amazingly."

Something of Allen's charm as a teacher lay in his voice. In his youth he had had a fine singing voice, but he strained it during his student days, and never sang again. Nor was he able to use it effectively in a large auditorium. But it was well suited to a small class room. It was, said Slattery, "one of those rare voices which once heard can never be forgotten." "There was always a magic compulsion in its soft low tones." Stewart Means described it as "peculiar in its softness, low and almost muffled, but flexible, expressive." "An exquisite conversational voice," said H. S. Nash.

Allen's gentle persuasive manner, his plump figure and his fresh round face led the students to dub him "Doctor Cherubicus."

"He had a curious habit," said E. T. Sullivan, '92, "of turning away from himself and towards the students the face of a little clock on the desk. They might watch the minutes of that hour, if they chose. He was dealing with the ages. And he was always surprised by the stroke of the bell. . . . Some of his lectures on the doctrine of the Trinity left his students almost breathless, and they went silently out as from a religious service."

"If you would understand an event or an institution," Allen would say, "find an adequate cause and a worthy explanation of it." "You have never got the true explanation of a man or a period until you have got an explanation which on the whole is creditable to humanity."

One of the most revealing comments on the quality of Allen's teaching is that by J. W. Suter, '85: "You would come into his class and he would, let us say, begin to talk about the Novatians. Up to that time you had probably not heard that there were such people as Novatians. Dr. Allen would explain their significance, and add, 'But there is one point about them still unexplained, a very important point, one that should be cleared up.' You would go out of the class feeling that the most important thing for the welfare of the Church was that this point about the Novatians should be cleared up, and that probably you were the man to do it."

Those who had not the good fortune to enter the School while Allen was still teaching, know him mainly through Slattery's life of him, and through his own books. His *Continuity of Christian Thought* has been characterized as "the most significant book of theology thus far written by an American." *Christian Institutions* and *Jonathan Edwards* are still books with which no student of either subject dare be unacquainted, and it is hardly conceivable that the *Life and Letters of Phillips Brooks* can ever be superseded.

Great as are his books, his former students insist that his lectures were greater. "The best thing," said Slattery, "an old pupil could say of any of his books was that it faintly reminded him of his lectures at the School." "When he had gone, many a man lost not only a master but a friend. He believed in men who were neither very good nor very clever; his generous belief kept them humble. . . . He gave them confidence in their task. And he left them always at the feet of the one Master, whom to serve was his own joy and freedom."

X

THE COMING OF DEAN HODGES

WHEN William Reed Huntington was asked to suggest someone for the vacant deanship he replied at once: "The author of a little book entitled *The Episcopal Church* — Dr. Hodges; it is the best argument for the Church that I know." J. W. Atwood, '82, later Bishop of Arizona, an intimate friend of Hodges, also urged his name, and Bishop-elect Lawrence was instrumental in getting him to come on from Pittsburgh in August, 1893, to preach in Rhode Island, stay with Atwood in Duxbury, Massachusetts, and spend a night in the home of Robert Treat Paine in Waltham. There Lawrence, Atwood, Hodges, and a few of the Trustees dined together. "Hodges," said Atwood, "shut his mouth like a clam, while Lawrence and I tried to rise to the occasion and talk as brilliantly as we could. Later, after we had gone upstairs, Hodges said, 'Why don't they elect you dean?'"

On October 4 they elected Hodges. At the end of that month he came to Cambridge to see the School and meet the Faculty and in mid-November he and Lawrence interviewed Dr. (later Bishop) Greer, J. P. Morgan, and others in New York in the hope of interesting them in the School. Dr. Greer suggested that the Board of Trustees be enlarged to include one or two New York men, a suggestion which bore fruit later.

It was almost the end of November before Hodges accepted. His hesitancy in doing so appears to have been due to the financial uncertainty with which the School faced the immediate future. Some day, when the residuary Reed legacy came to it, it would, it was hoped, be well off, but the health of Mr. Reed's widow was excellent and that of Mr. Reed's son's widow fabulous. Moreover, in comparison to Deans Gray and Lawrence, Hodges was at a financial disadvantage. They both had had independent means and both had turned back to the School much more than their salary of $2500 a year. Hodges had no independent means and he lacked those connections in and around Boston which had enabled Lawrence to raise almost $10,000 annually in gifts. He felt that $2500 a year was inadequate for his own needs and that the salaries of the professors were shameful. Steenstra and Allen, after twenty-five years of service, were receiving $2000; Nash the same; Kellner and Drown, $1250. He laid down as conditions of his acceptance that the salaries of the first three be raised $500, those of Kellner and Drown, $250; that he himself should have a wage adequate to the position he was expected to fill and the huge deanery he was expected to inhabit; and that the Trustees take measures to insure an income not only for these expenditures, but for the $10,000 annually needed for the current expense deficit.

In the face of a financial depression the Trustees went out for subscriptions. Robert Treat Paine, William Lawrence, each of the two daughters of Robert Means Mason, J. P. Morgan, and Mrs. Augustus Lowell all pledged $1000 a year for five years. Eight others pledged $500, and several more smaller amounts. With this assurance Hodges accepted. His salary was to be $4000.

George Hodges was thirty-seven years old when he was called to be Dean. He was the youngest dean the School has had. His deanship of twenty-five years was the longest in its history.

Hodges was descended from an old New England family, the first of his name to reach these shores arriving in 1633. Through his mother he was a descendant of both Miles

Standish and John Alden; hence a member of that group of people some of whose ancestors really came over in the Mayflower. He was born in 1856 at Rome, New York, whither his parents had moved from Taunton, Massachusetts. There he went to school until he was ready to enter Hamilton College, whence he graduated in 1877. After a year of teaching he entered Bishop Frederic Dan Huntington's short-lived theological school in Syracuse. Completing the studies supposed to represent a course of three years in one, he moved on to the Berkeley Divinity School, then at Middletown, Connecticut. On graduation in 1881 he became the assistant to Boyd Vincent at Calvary Church, Pittsburgh. In 1887 he was made associate rector and in 1889, when Vincent became Bishop of Southern Ohio, rector. In June, 1893, he was elected Bishop Coadjutor of Oregon, but declined. From Pittsburgh he was called to the School.

He was a preacher of distinction, a protagonist of Church unity, a leader in social betterment. "Calvary men and women," said a Pittsburgh layman, H. D. W. English, "under Dr. Hodges, began to take an interest in the city and its affairs. It was not long before the political powers that controlled the city called us 'that Damned Calvary Crowd.' We elected one of our vestry, the Hon. George W. Guthrie, mayor; we elected our senior warden to Congress; we elected another vestryman to be judge of the Orphans' Court. Under Mayor Guthrie an organization was formed called 'The Voters' League' which cleaned up graft in the Councils, putting eighteen councilmen in the penitentiary, and brought about a new charter for the city. . . . Dr. Hodges had the unique privilege of ministering to and influencing the social conscience of an entire city." He founded Kingsley House, a social settlement modeled after Toynbee Hall in London. He had a genius for getting people of all faiths working together.

A description of St. Chrysostom as a preacher, which Hodges gave later in his book on the Early Church, might well serve as a portrait of himself: "He was a small, slender man, without even the assistance of a strong voice. But what he said was clear and definite; nobody could mistake what he meant; he had emotion, he had humor, he had sympathy, he had passion. . . . And he addressed himself straight to common life."

He had also, before coming to Cambridge, shown his capacity as a teacher. His evening services had been largely devoted to instruction: he gave courses in doctrine and Church history and the Bible to crowded congregations. He had in extraordinary measure the gifts of simplification, of orderly presentation, of discerning, yet kindly judgment, together with an instinct for illustrative incident full of human interest, and, above all, a sense of humor.

His election to the deanship occurred the day before Lawrence's consecration to the episcopate. Lawrence wrote to him: "I cannot let the day of my consecration go by without writing you of my deep gratification that you have been elected Dean of this School. . . . I have been here as professor, Vice-Dean, and Dean almost nine years all together, and in all soberness I can say that it is the one position which in attractiveness, effectiveness, hope, opportunity, and joy, stands first in the Church."

After Hodges had visited the School and had been almost persuaded to accept, he wrote an article on it in his parish paper. "The opportunities," he said, "are great. The students are an unusually high class of men. . . . They are bound, by their training and character, to occupy the important parishes in the important cities. . . . The future of the Episcopal Church in this country depends greatly upon these young men. . . . In the congregation of the Chapel, too, are young Harvard men. They are also to be men of influence in the country. . . . The preacher, therefore, who stands in that pulpit, preaches to a hundred thousand people there represented by these future leaders.

"And then, of course, as a personal consideration, is the privilege of living in Cambridge. The people who live there think that it is ever so much more desirable as a place of residence than Pittsburgh. Though that may be due to their ignorance of Pittsburgh."

Not long after his settlement in Cambridge he wrote to a Pittsburgh friend: "These Boston people don't warm up to you — but they sometimes freeze on to you."

He never ceased to be mildly amused at the self-satisfaction of the neighborhood to which he had come to live. In 1909, when writing of the planting of the Church at Jamestown, Virginia, he noted some reasons why Plymouth had received more attention than Jamestown in our histories, and added: "The chief and prevailing disadvantage of Jamestown in its competition with Plymouth for the gratitude of good Americans lay in the fact that it was so far away from Boston. It was unhappily beyond the power of any Jamestown man to repeat the daily devotions of Mr. Emerson, who said that every morning, when he opened the shutters of his bed-chamber and looked out, he thanked God that he lived in so fair a world — and so near Boston."

He was tickled by an anecdote he got from Thomas Wentworth Higginson, and recorded it in his Journal — of the Boston child who asked, "Which came first, Adam and Eve or the Pilgrim Fathers?"

At the fiftieth anniversary of the School he recalled one of the considerations which had influenced him at the time of his call. He prefaced it by telling how he had recently set an examination question in which he gave ten names in the Bible and asked the students to write about any five of them. One of the ten, he said, was avoided by every student in the class. It was Jeshurun who "waxed fat and kicked." Jeshurun, said the Dean, was "the patron saint of the discontented," and he deemed it a happy omen that the students showed such ignorance of him. He went on to say: "I have always felt that the most conceited name which a parish could give itself is the name of 'All Saints.' You will bear me out, I know, in saying that there are parishes of various names which, if they were accurately named, would call themselves 'The Little Brothers and Sisters of Jeshurun.'

"That name applied to all the theological schools that I ever heard of until I came into acquaintance with this School. In all my experience a little knot of men getting together from any theological school would proceed to blaspheme the school; they would compare notes as to how much they did not learn when they were in the seminary. I never heard any man speak of this School in terms other than those of great respect and great affection. That was the first fact that came to my mind when I was asked to be Dean."

In addition to being Dean and pastor of the Chapel congregation, Hodges was Professor of Homiletics and Pastoral Care and Lecturer on Liturgics and Polity. He also gave courses on the English Bible. Although he did not teach Church History or Biography, he wrote several excellent books in these fields. "George Hodges," said Professor Bainton of Yale recently, "was the best popularizer of Church History we have ever had." Besides this, volumes of sermons, essays, confirmation instructions, books on the Bible, and Bible stories for children flowed from his pen in bewildering succession. His energy and his versatility were amazing. In these qualities he equalled if he did not surpass Francis Wharton.

During the last thirty-five years of his life he published thirty-four books, thirty of them during his deanship; he contributed chapters to two others, was joint author of three more, and author of at least fifty articles in *The Atlantic Monthly*, *The Ladies' Home Journal*, *The Outlook*, and

The Homiletic Review. His life of Christ for young people, *When the King Came*, achieved a sale of almost 28,000 copies; his *Three Hundred Years of the Episcopal Church in America* at least 30,000.

He was in continuous demand as a lecturer at Church conferences and preacher in college chapels. His published sermons were read by lay readers to congregations all over the land. He became in a very real sense the teacher of the whole Church and of an innumerable company outside it.

It was a wonder how he found time for it all. It has been said, truly enough, that he did not *find* time; he *made* it. He was the incarnation of order and industry, and he never seemed to be in a hurry. "People," he said, "are worn out not by the things which they do, but by the things they do not; the calls which are not made, the books which are not read, the stitches which are not taken, the letters which are not begun — these are the evil spirits which give us sleepless nights. Not one of them can live in an atmosphere of regulation. They flee before a systematic ordering of life as mice flee before the cat. The wise man who desires serenity and satisfaction will set about achieving them in the same sensible fashion in which he undertakes the erection of a house. He will draw up specifications. . . . It means a clear understanding between the clock and the conscience."

"Be systematic in the employment of time," he would say to the students. "This is the open secret of success."

It meant much to thoughtful students simply to have on the premises a man so disciplined, so productive, so widely recognized as the preceptor of the Church; it meant more to receive from him in class room and conference and chapel his rich fund of practical experience, his homely wisdom, his inclusive viewpoint, and to achieve, if one could, something of the superb clarity and quiet humor with which he presented them.

"The preacher," he would say, "should prepare himself

rather than his sermon. Clearness of vision depends on character. Bear in mind Chaucer's description of the parish priest: First he wrought and then he taught." "A minister is continually watched. People want to see if he is the kind of man they can trust and confide in and go to in sorrow." "Never scold anybody for not coming to church, or for anything else. Criticize as little as possible, praise as much as possible." "Do not let yourselves imagine that you are working very hard. Never have any idle moments. A minister should be ashamed to be found doing nothing." "Self seeking, looking out for a larger position is deplorable. The minister is the servant and ambassador of Jesus Christ. To get on is to do the work he *has* as well as he knows how."

As for preaching, his advice was: "Have something to say and then say it." "Preach so that the wife of the sexton can understand you as well as the wife of the Senior Warden." "The ideal sermon is a single important thought, stated, proved, illustrated, and applied." "Beware of somnolent delivery. Anyhow preach as if *you* thought it a good sermon." "Choose texts that will arouse attention and clinch your message. For example, when you want to preach on the Religious Responsibility of Men, take Matthew 20:20: 'Then came to Him the mother of Zebedee's children with her sons' — but where was Zebedee?'"

He cited the fisherman as an example for the minister: "One of the ministerial virtues of the fisherman is his patience. He casts his hook and waits. Another ministerial virtue of the fisherman is his preference for difficulty. He is interested in the elusive fish which hides among the rocks and views the bait with sophisticated indifference. . . . The fisherman makes use of variety. He knows that while some fish like worms, others prefer frogs, and others flies. . . . . He has no theory of a standard fish-food which the fish must take or leave. Still less is he disposed to infer the fishes' appetite from his own, and to offer as bait the sort of thing he himself had for breakfast — one of the commonest errors of the clergy. His question is, What will the fish take? And he finds the answer by continual experiment." His readiness of wit and aptness of illustration were proverbial. At an Alumni dinner when Bishop William Lawrence spoke of the Dean as simple and transparent, the Dean retorted by telling how King Charles I, in a stained glass window in the Church of the Evangelists, Philadelphia, was wont to look up at the statue of William Penn on the tower of City Hall and say, "William, people look up to you, but they see through me!"

Speaking of the function of music in the services of the Church, he paraphrased the Parable of the Sower: "The seed is the word of God. Those by the wayside are they that hear. Then cometh the anthem and taketh away the word out of their hearts."

When the Class of 1904, at its tenth anniversary, presented his portrait to the School, he looked at it quizzically and said: "I have seen this picture all too often, and whenever I look at it I agree with Oliver Wendell Holmes that a face is not an ornament but a convenience."

Not the least of his contributions to his students was his own contagious spirit of comprehension, of eagerness to understand an alien viewpoint, of charitable judgment, of willingness to coöperate in every good cause, no matter what its denominational or party name. One of his repeated pieces of advice was that if a man was a low churchman he should make friends of high churchmen; if he were a high churchman he should make friends of low churchmen; for by intimate knowledge of persons could the good in their positions best be appreciated.

Two years before his death he wrote an article on Archbishop Cranmer. You may not agree with his characterization of Cranmer, but whether you do or not, you would recognize Hodges himself, had you known him, in this characterization:

"He was an open-minded, friendly person, whose preference was for agreement rather than disagreement, and he saw that there was good on both sides. . . . He had the humble mind of the wise scholar. . . . He perceived that the conservatives were right: the men of the new learning parted with him at that point. He perceived also that the progressives were right: the men of the old learning declined to go with him down that road. This perplexing situation was further complicated by the fact that he perceived himself to be liable to error. He changed his mind. . . .

"The consequences were bad for Cranmer, but they were good every way for the Book of Common Prayer. This gift of sympathy made it an inclusive book. . . .

"Cranmer's spirit has not always prevailed in the counsels of the Anglican Church. It was forgotten when high churchmen were turned out in the days of Elizabeth, and when low churchmen were turned out in the days of Charles II. But there have always been some to remember it, and there are now many such — comprehensive churchmen, of whom it can be said that the Kingdom of God is within them, for the unity of the contending churches is realized already in the hospitality of their own souls."

XI

THE HERESY OF DEAN HODGES

Heresy," Dean Hodges was fond of saying, "is partial truth. All profound truth has two sides. It has a nearer side which the mind may apprehend. It has also a farther side, beyond all human apprehension, extending into infinity. The heretic is the man who, having attained certain definite ideas of truth, cries, 'Now I know it all.' The heretic has a complete system of theology. This also is the refutation of heresy. There can be no complete solution of any equation which contains the factor of infinity."

Little prone as Dean Hodges was ever to cry "Now I know it all," he did not escape the imputation of heresy. Indeed, by simply coming to Cambridge he laid himself open to that charge. Coincident with his arrival an anonymous writer in the *Church Eclectic* asserted, "That School at Cambridge is heretical all the way through," and buttressed his assertion by observing that Allen was a disciple of F. D. Maurice, whose theology was "the denial of everything that the Catholic Church has ever held sacred."

Hodges began his deanship on the feast of the Epiphany, 1894. In June of that year twenty-two men graduated.[1] That was the largest graduating class, up to that time, in the history of the School. It was the largest the School was destined to have until 1942. It was also a class which, in the persons of several of its members, was to bring distinction

[1] The present Catalogue names twenty-four, but two of them, who were special students in 1894, received certificates *honoris causa* eight years later.

to the School, but at the time of its graduation it increased the School's repute for heretical pravity.

Owing to the large number of men taking canonical examinations in Massachusetts, the examiners, instead of examining as a board, separated, and each examiner questioned a few of the men individually. Two of the students, who fell into the hands of the Rev. A. St. John Chambre, felt that his questions savored of the nature of a heresy hunt. He undoubtedly regarded himself as a watch-dog of orthodoxy: he had not only been suspicious of the theology of Phillips Brooks, but also of that of Father A. C. A. Hall of the Society of St. John the Evangelist, and had opposed the confirmation of both of them for the episcopate. On the other hand the students in question were noted for having a dogmatic chip on their shoulder and doubtless behaved toward the examiner in a cocky and irritating manner.

While not denying the doctrine of the Virgin Birth, they declined to affirm it as essential to the Incarnation. They declared that they would believe in Jesus Christ as Very God of Very God even if the initial chapters of Matthew and Mark should be shown to lack historical trustworthiness. This the examiner regarded as heresy.

Bishop Lawrence, after conference with the two men, concluded that their position was admissible and expressed his willingness to ordain them. The examiner, however, was a member of the Standing Committee, and the Committee deferred its recommendation of them for ordination. At this stage of the proceedings the School graduation occurred, and the "heretics" received their degrees with the rest of their class. Subsequently, one of them, being examined by the full board of examiners, was unanimously given satisfactory testimonials and was ordained; the other, after further study abroad, decided not to enter the ministry and never came up for reëxamination.

All of this might have passed off without further comment had not the Boston *Transcript* published an editorial headed "Unitarian Episcopalism," in which the writer, pointing to the cases of these two men, contended that "the flow of doctrine" in the Episcopal Church was "in one direction, almost in the channel of early Unitarianism."

This was the signal for a deluge of letters, articles, and editorials on "the Massachusetts Case," as it was called, in both the religious and the secular press, not to mention numerous sermons and pamphlets, in which the School, the diocese, and the Bishop were charged with betraying the faith. The School was especially faulted for having given the two men their degrees. To this the Dean replied that since they had completed all their work satisfactorily there had been no question of withholding them. But had the question been raised, the Faculty, seeing that the Bishop, after investigation, had declared the men worthy of ordination, "would no doubt have upheld the episcopal authority."

The discussion culminated in a pronouncement of the House of Bishops or rather of a committee of six of them. The bishops met in October, 1894, to elect a missionary bishop. After adjournment they sat informally "in council" (a procedure which has no canonical standing) and appointed a committee of six to prepare a Pastoral Letter on the questions which were agitating the Church. In this letter it was maintained that belief in the miraculous physical birth of Christ is essential to a belief in the Incarnation; that it is derogatory to the Holy Ghost "to suggest that any other than the original sense of the creeds may be lawfully held and taught"; and that "fixedness of interpretation is of the essence of the creeds."

The joy with which this was hailed by those who held the School in disfavor was somewhat dampened by the statement of Henry Codman Potter, one of the six bishops who signed it, that "the Pastoral Letter has undoubtedly no conciliar authority, and may be said, if anybody chooses to say so, to have little more value than is expressed in the more or less close consensus of opinion of some half dozen individuals."

Controversy continued for some time, but the School wisely refrained from taking further part in it. In June, 1895, the Dean, in his annual report, although making no mention of "the Massachusetts Case" or the Bishops' Pastoral Letter, clearly had both in mind. He spoke of the mature methods of instruction at the School, saying, "Men are taught to think; and thinking is a perilous process. . . . Nevertheless, we feel that we are set here to fit men for ministry in this present generation. . . . If we could send our students to their work equipped only with the formulas of Church authority, our task would be easy. . . . A submissive mind and a confident manner and several orthodox authorities committed well to memory would suffice the young priest for his work. We cannot thus construe our duty. We must teach our men the truth together with the reasons for believing it. Every endeavor of the scholars, every labor of the critics, every utterance of the men by whom the Holy Spirit speaks to-day, every new book, every most recent question, we must bring into the class room. . . . At the same time we consider that our task is not so much the discovery as the interpretation of truth. We are in search not of new truth, but of new meanings and applications of that eternal and unchanging truth which was revealed in the words and in the life of Jesus Christ. . . . We lay great emphasis, indeed, on scholarship, and stand for the need of a trained and equipped ministry, but we consider character to be the supreme essential of the Christian minister."

Not only did the School's teaching in the field of Biblical Criticism rouse suspicions of its orthodoxy, the Dean's zeal for interdenominational coöperation laid him open to censure. In 1896 he invited the ministers of all denominations in Cambridge to a conference in St. John's Chapel. About thirty came. One of the speakers was Professor Francis G. Peabody of Harvard, a Unitarian. This evoked an outburst from the Rev. William B. Frisbie of the Church of the Advent. "Can it be imagined," he wrote to *The Living Church*, "by those who live outside of Boston — a disciple of Arius instructing priests of the Catholic Church? . . . Was the Council of Nicaea held in vain? Must the work of Athanasius count for nothing?"

Said the Dean: "Year by year the Episcopal Church broadens its sympathies and becomes less ecclesiastical and more Christian, and in the process some of the old bottles are sure to burst with more or less of an explosion."

"Some people," he wrote later, "seem to be a little afraid of going into meetings of other ministers lest they shall find out that we are no better than they are." He counselled against the tendency to assume that the truth is to be found only in one's own denomination by saying, "It is well to avoid the imposition that the boy played upon his companions when he sold them tickets for admission to his mother's front yard to see the eclipse."

In 1901 a generation of students who evidently knew nothing of Father Frisbie's earlier attitude invited him to speak to the "My Neighbor Club." "I resolved some time ago," he replied, "to have nothing whatever to do with that School, as I believe it to be wrongly constituted and a source of discredit to the Church."

With this, Bishop Nicholson of Milwaukee was in hearty agreement. In 1900 when Dr. Nash was seriously ill, Joseph Henry Thayer, professor in the Harvard Divinity School, author of the *Greek-English Lexicon of the New Testament*, and one of the most distinguished of New Testament scholars, conducted one of Nash's courses. He did so out of friendship for Nash and without salary. Bishop Nicholson wrote to *The Living Church* that Dr. Thayer

teaching in an Episcopal school was "a novelty sufficient to
disturb the peace of mind of all loyal churchmen," and
averred that the time had come for the General Convention
to take control of all our seminaries. He admitted that he
had assumed that Dr. Thayer was a Unitarian, but on hearing that he was a "liberal Congregationalist," said he could
see no difference. Mr. Morehouse agreed editorially with
Bishop Nicholson that the situation was dreadful, but said
he was sure that neither Bishop Lawrence nor Dean Hodges
could help it. It was due to the School's lay trustees, who
did not know any better!

In 1906 Biblical Criticism again came to the fore. Some
seventy-five clergy and laity issued a printed statement in
which they called the attention of the Church to a letter
which had been circulated in England over the signatures
of 1700 clergy concerning the critical study of the New
Testament and which, among other things, registered the
conviction of the signers that they ought not to "build the
faith of souls primarily upon details of New Testament narrative, the historical validity of which must ultimately be
determined in the court of trained research." Among the
signers of the American statement were Dean Hodges, Professors Allen and Nash, the Trustees, Robert Treat Paine
and Richard Henry Dana, as well as several graduates of the
School.

Dr. Algernon S. Crapsey, who was then under fire because of his views, at once hailed this as a vindication. The
next year Mr. George Foster Peabody, the Brooklyn philanthropist, who was one of the signers of this statement,
and who had paid the expenses of the defense in the Crapsey
trial, sent copies of Dr. Allen's *Freedom in the Church*,
which had just been published, to all Episcopal clergymen.
This gave rise to rumors of a "well organized attempt," led
by the School, "to capture the forthcoming General Convention in the interest of Crapseyism," as well as to a

proposal by Bishop Grafton of Fond du Lac that the Convention ought to place all theological schools under the supervision of the bishops in the department or province in which they were situated. He frankly said that he had the Cambridge School in mind.

Dean Hodges assured the Church that there were no sympathizers with Dr. Crapsey in the School, "except in so far as we don't believe in ecclesiastical trials. We sympathize with him on that score but on no other. We are not in sympathy with his theology." There were many, however, who refused to believe this.

Dr. Allen used to say that he did not like to attend Church conventions because they always sang "The Church's One Foundation," and when they came to the line, "By heresies distressed," everybody looked at him. One lady left the Chapel congregation because, she said, "Dean Hodges was a Unitarian, Dr. Nash an atheist, and Mr. Drown impossible."

It may be that the phenomenally small enrollment in 1907–08, namely twenty-seven in the whole School, was in part due to the widespread suspicion of the School's orthodoxy at the time. Yet the opening of the next School year saw one of the largest entering groups in its history — twenty-four. Doubtless the Dean was correct when he said, "These ebbs and floods seem to have little relation to the current controversies."

What the School's fearless consideration of the problems of Biblical criticism meant to the students of the time may be judged by a statement made by H. C. Robbins, '03, fourteen years after his graduation:

"I began my study for the ministry in what is perhaps the most conservative Protestant seminary in this country [the Princeton Theological Seminary]. The atmosphere was that of aggressive orthodoxy. . . . The 'Higher Critic' was depicted as an enemy lurking in ambush. . . .

"I went from this great conservative seminary to the Episcopal Theological School in Cambridge. To sum up the transition in a word, it was like stepping out of the eighteenth century into the nineteenth, out of the world and thought of Jonathan Edwards into the world and thought of Frederick Robertson and Frederick Maurice, of Horace Bushnell and of Phillips Brooks. The great note of this liberal school was the note of reality. Its atmosphere was the atmosphere of freedom. Its ultimate allegiance was not to letter but to spirit, not to book, creed, or institution, but to the living Christ, who by his Spirit still guides his people into ever unfolding truth. And that truth was not looked upon as a frail thing, to be defended by human ingenuity, but as something so mighty that all it demanded of us was loyalty, and courage to follow it in whatever direction it might guide. I cannot put into words the relief to mind and heart and spirit which accompanied this transition. It was, and is still, the deepest religious experience of my life."

XII

HODGES AND THE TRADITIONS

THREE months after beginning his work at the School the Dean wrote for his former parish paper: "Some of you may be interested to know how life goes on in these parts. Every day at half past eight Morning Prayer is said in the Chapel. All the students are present, there are always some people from the congregation, and the six professors in their surplices march in picturesque procession.[1] The students sing the responses and chant a Psalm in the Psalter for the day. The music is all Gregorian, which is excellently adapted to men's voices. Then come lectures until one o'clock, though not at all the hours for all the professors. . . . At five o'clock every day Evening Prayer is said. During Lent we have addresses — on Mondays and Saturdays by the Dean, on Tuesdays by the seniors, on Wednesdays and Fridays by the professors, and on Thursdays by the Cambridge clergy. The church is two-thirds as full at many of these services as it is on Sunday."

It is small wonder that he found that the students "complained at the number of sermons to which they have been compelled to listen." A few years later it became the custom to have a sermon by a senior one evening each week, an address by the Dean on another and, in Lent, an additional address by a visiting preacher.

[1] The "picturesque procession" continued until the early years of Dean Washburn, when the present custom was adopted, namely, for the one (or two) who conduct the service to enter vested in surplice and tippet (or stole for Communion), the rest of the Faculty, in gowns, taking their places individually before service.

Although simplicity was one of Dean Hodges' most conspicuous characteristics, he found the chancel of the Chapel too bare and the services too simple even for his modest taste. He secured the gift of a cross for the altar and introduced the wearing of colored stoles. He also provided for the celebration of Holy Communion on saints' days, and full Morning Prayer on other days. Hitherto there had been one weekday communion each month and in Morning Prayer the opening sentences and the Venite had been omitted, only one Psalm used and one lesson.[2]

The students were distressed at these innovations, especially at colored stoles and lengthened Morning Prayer. One of the seniors, C. L. Slattery, went to the Dean early in May to protest, and, on the morning after Ascension Day, the Dean found a slip of paper pinned to his white stole on which was written, "*See* Acts 28:14." When looked up this read, "And so we went toward Rome." A quarter of a century later, J. B. Dunn, '94, then rector of St. Paul's Church, Lynchburg, Virginia, confessed that he had been the culprit. The anonymous Scripture reference was followed in a few days by a signed petition in which the students expressed their opinion "that a return to the simplicity and freedom in the Chapel services is desirable." Among the twenty-one signers were the future Presiding Bishop James DeWolf Perry, the future Bishops Slattery, Thurston, and Roots, and the future Dean Washburn!

Not the least of Dean Hodges' qualities was his capacity for silence. When a student delegation brought him the petition, he read it and, without a syllable of comment, looked up cheerfully and waited for them to speak. Dean Washburn, who was one of the delegation, says he has never

[2] He also provided for an early Communion every Sunday. Under Dean Lawrence there had been a late celebration on the first and third Sundays. These services were primarily for the Chapel congregation; most of the students had Sunday duties elsewhere. Candles were not used on the altar till about 1924, under Dean Washburn.

experienced such an all embracing quiet. It routed the delegation. They left without a word, and the services went on as the Dean had begun them. In the Dean's diary appears this entry: "May 9, 1894. Was waited upon today by a delegation consisting of Slattery, Hoopes, and Washburn, who wanted a return to the former directness and simplicity of the service. Had a pleasant interview with them."

"How vividly I recall the Dean's coming to the School," said J. B. Dunn many years later, "and the reckless way in which he handled what we were pleased to call the traditions. We deemed him less dangerous when he expressed a desire to make the acquaintance of a dish new to him, called 'hot dog.' Thurston, Kobayashi, Sargent, and I called for him late one night, and midnight found the new Dean and four of his seniors in a lunch wagon at Harvard Square."

When the Dean thought the students slack in attendance at chapel he posted the notice: "*See* Joshua 3:1." They found, "And Joshua rose early in the morning." One youth countered, undoubtedly to the amusement of the Dean, with, "*See* John 11:12," which reads, "If he sleep he shall do well."

Under June 18, 1895, in Dean Hodges' diary occurs this idyllic paragraph: "To-day the senior class and I took an electric car at nine o'clock and went to Arlington where we took the train for Lexington. We went to the historic Green and to the house where Paul Revere awakened Hancock and Adams. And then to church where I celebrated Holy Communion and talked a long time to the men on their ordination vows. Then we took our big lunch basket and a bucket of water and a pail of ice and went out into the woods, where we had a pleasant quiet time till the two-thirty train."

Shortly before, the Dean had made this note in his diary: "Some of the men seem quite lacking in appreciation of the church services. Another fault of the men I learned from the bursar is that they do not pay their bills for room and board. This is an interesting condition of things: students for the ministry who do not care to come to church, and who do not pay their bills."

How many were reckoned in these categories we do not know, but we can be sure that they received appropriate attention from the Dean. At the same time there appears to have been a considerable amount of what might be called extra-chapel activity among the students. During Advent and Lent they held a daily compline service. Then there was the St. John's Society and the My Neighbor Club, with its frequent devotional meetings. There was also the Foreign Missionary Reading Club, begun in 1894, for prayer for and study of foreign missions.

The formation of this last group was by no means the beginning of missionary interest in the School, although it marked an intensification of that interest. As early as 1878 Theodosius S. Tyng, '74, had gone to Japan. E. R. Woodman, '80, followed. Both worked there for almost thirty years. In 1887 the St. John's Society was organized for the purpose of fostering concern for missions. The presence of J. H. Kobayashi, '94, the first Oriental student in the School, did much to increase this concern, and L. H. Roots, '96, returning from a Student Volunteer Convention in 1894, led in the launching of the Foreign Missionary Reading Club, which, in his senior year, was renamed the St. Paul's Club.

While the St. John's Society listened to missionary speakers, the St. Paul's Club studied mission fields, non-Christian religions, and missionary biography. It continued to meet, sometimes weekly, sometimes bi-weekly, increasing its attendance from ten to twenty, until 1905, when it was absorbed, together with the My Neighbor Club, into the St. John's Society. During the period of its independent existence there were eleven men in the School who later served in foreign lands. Roots was the first graduate to become a foreign missionary bishop — of Hankow, China, in 1904. K. G. Tourian, '05, missionary of the Armenian Church in India, and Bishop of Trebizond, Turkey, was the School's first and as yet only martyr. He was killed by the Turks in 1915.

The peak enrollments in Hodges' deanship were in 1895, when there were fifty-one students, and in 1913, when there were fifty-two. The average for his first twenty-two years, namely 1894–1916, was exactly forty.

Many of the School's "immemorial customs" originated in Dean Hodges' days. Holy Communion on saints' days and colored stoles have already been mentioned. In 1909 the Thursday morning Holy Communion, in weeks when there was no saints' day, came in. The restriction of the use of stoles to the Communion and the wearing of the scarf or tippet at Morning and Evening Prayer dates from 1912.

Saturday classes were introduced in 1896. Monday mornings were kept free until 1902 when classes late in the morning first appeared. They gradually increased until, in 1910, Monday was like any other day. In 1906 two semesters replaced the three terms of the previous school year.

The wearing of academic gowns on "special occasions" began shortly before Dean Hodges' time. In 1889 the Faculty, in 1892 the students first wore them at Commencement. In 1895 Dean Hodges proposed that the students wear them every day in chapel, but the Faculty voted "No." In 1900 they voted "Yes."

Hoods did not appear so early. In 1886 some of the graduates in Canada urged the School to adopt a hood, but nothing was done about it. Hoods were not yet the fashion in Cambridge. Shortly after William Lawrence joined the Faculty he had occasion, in Dean Gray's absence, to welcome the Dean's brother, the Warden of Racine College, who came to preach in the Chapel. To Lawrence's wonderment the guest took something red out of his bag. He explained that it was a hood. "Oh," said Lawrence, "I have heard that some of the small colleges in the west are adopting them." "Is there any objection to my wearing it?" asked the guest. "None," said Lawrence. When Dean Gray heard of it he exclaimed, "Why didn't you prevent it? I'll never let him in the Chapel again!"

Hodges, early in his own deanship, wore a hood at a matriculation service. Dr. Steenstra asked him why he wore it. "Because it was given to me," said the Dean. The next day in class Steenstra solemnly dictated the following, enunciating each word deliberately, as was his custom, so it could be taken down verbatim: "The combination of the late priestly history with the earlier composite prehistoric histories resulted in the first six books of the Old Testament. The next thing we'll see will be the Dean wearing cap and bells if someone gives them to him."

In 1897 the Faculty voted to adopt a School hood, and the secretary, Dr. Kellner, was careful to record that "Professor Steenstra, the only member of the Faculty not present at this meeting, concurred in this vote." It was not the hood we now have. Although conforming to the intercollegiate pattern, the lining was to be purple. Two years later a red chevron was voted. In 1901 the color was changed to white with a chevron of "divinity red," as we now have it. Dr. Steenstra's consent to all this must undoubtedly have been secured by an assurance that he would never have to wear a hood himself, for it was not till 1909, two years after his retirement, that the Faculty voted to wear hoods over their surplices at matriculation.

In 1899 the present School seal was adopted. The first seal, appearing on documents in 1880, if not before, was simply an open book encircled with the words *Mane Verbum Domini in Aeternum*. In 1887 an elaboration of this, surmounted by a mitre, came into use. Dean Hodges was dissatisfied with it and, after studying the seals of the English colleges, devised the present version with the help of Mr. F. Apthorp Foster, a son of one of the Visitors. "He put the seal in shape," said the Dean, "from a rough design I gave him. He suggested the red cross on the shield. I made the motto, *Veritas et Vita*. The open book connects us with our original seal; *Veritas* suggests our neighborhood to Harvard; and the addition of the words *et Vita* denotes our purpose, which is to apply truth to life." Outside the shield were the words *Justificatio ex fide*.

Dean Lawrence in his last year at the School invited the Alumni to lunch on the pre-Lenten Quiet Day. Dean Hodges did so again in 1896 and continued to do so regularly thereafter, thus establishing what many regard as the pleasantest Alumni occasion in the year. The mid-winter dinner was not added till 1909,[3] the year in which, at the suggestion of the Alumni, the *Bulletin* was first issued.

The Alumni Prayer, written by Dean Hodges, was first used in 1899, in a farewell service for Sakai, '97:

"O Lord, our heavenly Father, the source and perfection of all strength; Look, we pray thee, with thy blessing upon our brethren who have gone out of this school into the work of the ministry; grant unto them the spirit of wisdom that they may teach thy people thine eternal truth, and the spirit of holiness that they may go before them and lead them into thine everlasting kingdom; through Jesus Christ our Lord. *Amen*."

It was the Dean who suggested that the Trustees should

[3] On the night *before* the Quiet Day; since 1921 on the night of the Quiet Day. In 1924 the afternoon Faculty paper was added. The June meeting and dinner came the afternoon and evening before Commencement through 1922; after that on Commencement Day. From 1878 to 1907 Commencement and the ordination of deacons were combined. Beginning with 1908 they were separated. In 1921 the Commencement Holy Communion was moved up to 8 A.M. and a Commencement service compiled by J. W. Suter, '85, was used at 11 A.M. This is the form still used. The Commencement breakfast for the graduating class at the deanery was instituted by Dean Hodges.

set apart a room which any alumnus might occupy and at the same time take meals at the refectory as the guest of the School. He hoped that it might be furnished in memory of a former Trustee. The son of Judge Bennett acted on this suggestion and "the Bennett Room" came into being in 1902.

The School Hymn, written by R. T. Henshaw, '07, was first used at Matriculation in 1906. It was sung to the tune of "For thee, O dear, dear country." At the Commencement in 1907 the tune composed by Dudley Tyng, '09 was used.

The Christmas play was introduced by the lively class of 1911 in their junior year. It has, ever since, been one of the School's most delightful annual functions.

Baseball has long been a popular pastime, but it seems to have flourished with peculiar luxuriance during the two decades before the first world war. A School team was organized each spring and games played with the Harvard law students, with neighboring seminaries, with Groton and St. Mark's Schools, and with the Alumni. Dr. Drown umpired, and the Faculty cheered. The annual excursions to Groton and St. Mark's were gala outings in which the whole school participated. Said the Dean at the fortieth anniversary of the School: "We have had the best baseball team that the School has ever had — I say 'ever had' somewhat inadvertently, because it is insisted by some that the best team was that in which three of the places were filled by Dr. Nash, Dr. Drown, and Dean Lawrence — but we have had a series of great victories this year over the Socinians and Anabaptists. I think that the boys took a little unfair advantage of the Baptists, playing the game with them on a day when it sprinkled."

Baseball has continued as a spring diversion to the present, but the games at a distance, with Groton and St. Mark's and with other seminaries, have been less frequent during the past decade. The game with the Alumni is still an annual event, although, to the disgust of the latter, the students in recent years have preferred a soft ball to a hard one.[4]

Some of the customs of Dean Hodges' time have not been continued. One was Sunday evening hymn singing at the deanery. Another was Founders' Day, an annual occasion commemorating the founder and other benefactors and at the same time affording an opportunity for people in and around Boston to become acquainted with the School. The first was October 22, 1908, when 500 guests came. There was an address by the Bishop, a reception, and a "collation in the refectory." Although an annual event, the date varied according to the choice of the Faculty. The last seems to have been in 1914.

Another custom beginning early in Hodges' deanship was the setting apart of the late afternoon and the evening of Friday as times for social gatherings. There was tea in the faculty homes in the afternoon; each faculty household had four or five students at dinner; and throughout the evening students would call, often in groups, making the rounds of the faculty houses. There might be games or charades or singing or, in the years when faculty daughters were growing up, dancing. Dean Hodges often delighted us by reading aloud O. Henry's stories. Some of the pleasantest memories of my student days are connected with these Friday evenings. It need hardly be added that their charm was due quite as much to the hostesses as to the hosts, and alumni recall with unvarying delight the friendly hospitality of Mrs. Hodges, Mrs. Washburn, Mrs. Nash, Mrs. Kellner, Miss Amy Drown — "Aunt Amy" as many students affectionately called her — and, after Dr. Drown's marriage, Mrs. Drown.

---

[4] Almost every year since 1931 a basket ball team has been organized and has engaged in inter-school games. Touch-football, for exercise, has been played in the afternoons in the fall for two decades or more.

Dean Hodges' conception of the functions of a theological school as well as his realization of its limitations finds expression in a sermon he preached in St. Bartholomew's, New York, in 1903:

"The first element of a successful ministry is *religion*. . . . The theological school cannot make the minister a man of religion; but it can surround him for three impressionable years with the atmosphere of religion. By its daily services, by its frequent Communions, by its counsels and admonitions, by its reverent handling of divine truth, by its common conduct, it can help the minister to be a man of religion. It can start him right. And it can inform the man who is lacking in the spirit of religion that he has no place in the Christian ministry.

"The second element of a right ministry is *health*. The minister must be able to work hard and long. It is true that the saints were seldom very well; and so strong is the old tradition that it is still a little hard to imagine a sun-burned saint. So much the worse for the saints. That was one of their shortcomings. . . . Here, again, the theological school cannot help much. It can, however, discourage infirm persons from coming in; and it can provide its students with such a novitiate of good, hard, steady work, that the weak brethren cannot endure it, but must give out and give up.

"A third quality is *sense*. . . . The theological school cannot teach men sense. I wish it could. But it can help them to be sensible. It can give them good advice, again and again repeated, for three years, and that is something.

"A fourth element in an efficient ministry is *knowledge* and the ability to impart it. The Christian minister is a teacher of religion. . . . I mean the sense of certainty of God. . . . To be sure of God is the secret of abiding peace and joy.

"How shall the preacher be trained to teach religion? By

his own experience of life, by his intercourse with the Eternal, by his personal acquaintance with man and with God; into all of which a door is opened wide at the school of theology. There he learns to read and interpret the Word of God; there he is put in possession of the course of history, that he may understand the way and the will of God. There he studies the masters of theology, that he may the better know the truth of God. . . .

"No school can of itself make a man a preacher; but a good school can train any intelligent man to express himself simply and shortly. It can impress upon him the fact that no congregation likes long sermons, and that no sermon seems so long as that in which the preacher wanders slowly here and there with no apparent destination. No school can make a man a good executive; but a competent school will teach him the methods of parochial administration. It will inform him how to conduct a Sunday School, how to prepare persons for confirmation, how to organize a parish for effective work, how to make useful visits among his people, and how to live at peace with his vestry."

He often reminded the students that the Chapel was the heart of the School's life, where they were to come "morning and evening, day by day, into the reproaching and compelling presence of the cross." Next in importance was the classroom: "One of the greatest needs of the Christian religion today is that of a convincing ministry to educated men. . . . No confidence in the grace of orders will persuade thoughtful persons to listen with appreciation while young men in surplices tell them what they ought to believe without telling them why they ought to believe it. . . . When the man comes who makes faith possible, who makes truth clear, they salute him as the wise men of old saluted the revealing star. . . . To learn the truth so that you yourselves possess it — so that it enters into your soul — and then in the might of that precious possession to go and teach your fellow-man — this is the great achievement for the sake of which a school of theology exists. . . .

"Unhappily, the habit of adoration does not always make men humble, nor does the habit of reflection make them considerate. . . . Out of the benediction of the Chapel, out of the inspiration of the class-room, you will come — what kind of man? When your instructors and your companions have answered that question in the silence of their own hearts, they have thereby prophesied your ministerial future. For your usefulness in the ministry depends, not on your learning and not on your sanctity, but on the way in which you are able to bring your wisdom and your goodness into relation with the lives of others. The most ancient of all arts is the art of living with others; and you have got to be a master of it. . . . The social life of the school is thus a means of grace as well as a means of pleasure. It is a preparation for effective service."

When speaking of the neighborhood of the School the Dean observed: "A strong Puritan preference for directness and simplicity, which is breathed in by young men from the academic atmosphere of the place, makes artificial and conventional religion ridiculous."

XIII

TRUSTEES, VISITORS, AND FACULTY

ROBERT C. WINTHROP, last of the original Trustees and President of the Board since 1882, died near the close of 1894. He was succeeded as President by Judge E. H. Bennett who held the office till 1898. Then came Robert Treat Paine, till 1910, and William H. Lincoln, till 1925. Winthrop was a Trustee for twenty-seven years; Bennett for sixteen; Paine for twenty-seven; Lincoln for twenty-eight. Throughout the whole of Hodges' deanship and beyond, Harcourt Amory was Secretary of the Trustees and Richard Henry Dana Treasurer.

In the first year of Mr. Lincoln's presidency the Fundamental Articles were revised, permitting the selection of some of the Trustees from outside the Diocese of Massachusetts, thus carrying out the suggestion made by Dr. Greer eighteen years before.

In the same year there was a reorganization of the Board of Visitors. After their rebuff by the Trustees in 1885, when they sought more power in the administration of the School, their meetings as well as their visitations became less and less frequent, until, from 1905 to 1910, they did not meet or visit at all, or if they did they kept no records. They may well have argued that since their President, Bishop Lawrence, was living beside the School and in intimate touch with it, there was little need for them to be concerned about it.

The Faculty, however, were concerned about the Visitors. Professors Nash and Washburn, acting as "a committee to consider the continuance, make-up, and duties of the

Board of Visitors," reported that the duties for which Visitors had originally been designed, namely to keep an eye on the morals, the theology, and the teaching methods of the School, were now being fulfilled by other agencies. "The School lies open on every side to the knowledge and inquisition of its neighbors. If there is anything morally wrong with it, the Bishop, the Church at large, the Trustees, will quickly be informed. . . . Again the Church has ample means of detecting heresy in our School. The Bishops, through their examining chaplains, serve this end. A smelling committee is needless." As for reform in teaching methods, the spur to this "comes from the educational world at large, and particularly from the university world." "The Board of Visitors," they concluded, "is a sort of theological appendix." However, it should not be abolished, but should be "stripped of all power" and made a purely advisory body. (The committee evidently supposed that the Visitors had some power.) It would be well to select the clerical members of the Board from the Alumni, and membership, instead of being permanent, should change continually, one member being retired every year.

This report was first submitted to Bishop Lawrence, who questioned the wisdom of appointing alumni. "Academic institutions are liable to breed in on themselves," he said. "It would be well to have some men who have had their education elsewhere."

The Trustees adopted the suggestion of a changing membership and, in order to remove even the appearance of "power," deleted from the Fundamental Articles the phrase, "they shall correct and reform all abuses."

Since then the Visitors have "visited" with some degree of regularity at least once a year, and have frequently made suggestions from which both Trustees and Faculty have profited. Said Dean Hodges: "It is for our advantage, and for the good of the Church, that a considerable number of persons, rectors of parishes and eminent laymen, should come into relation with our work. We need their counsel."

For the first thirteen years of Hodges' deanship the Faculty consisted of himself, Steenstra, Allen, Nash, Kellner, and Drown. Then in 1907 Steenstra retired; in 1908 Allen died. They were the last of the original Faculty. The entire Alumni body had been their pupils. That their places could be filled seemed a stark impossibility. As one alumnus put it, the idea of a genuine successor to Allen was "but the thought of the shadow of reality." But the situation was met triumphantly.

In 1907 P. M. Rhinelander was called to the newly created chair of the History of Religion and Missions; in 1908 H. B. Washburn succeeded Allen; in the same year H. E. W. Fosbroke became lecturer and the next year Professor of the History and Religion of Israel. Thus by the almost simultaneous appointment of these three men the Faculty was made stronger than before. Rhinelander was a stimulating teacher, Fosbroke a great teacher, and it was soon evident that Allen's mantle had fallen on the right shoulders.

Hodges, Nash, Kellner, Drown, Rhinelander, Washburn, and Fosbroke made a truly remarkable faculty — but not for long. In 1911 Rhinelander was elected Bishop of Pennsylvania; in 1912 Nash died; in 1916 Fosbroke resigned to become, the next year, Dean of the General Seminary. It is small wonder that the Alumni, gathered in St. Louis at the time of the General Convention in 1916, spoke of "the crisis through which the School is passing" and evinced "a general feeling of concern." "Where," they asked, "is the School we knew?"

That the School at the same time was trying out a group of unknown youngsters, doubtless increased the Alumni's concern: W. F. Gookin, '05, began instructing in the New Testament in 1911; J. A. Muller, '10, in Church History in 1914; J. T. Addison, '13, in the History of Religion and Missions in 1915; N. B. Nash, '15, in the New Testament in 1916.[1]

A substantial addition to the Faculty came in 1917, when W. H. P. Hatch, '02, was called from the General Seminary to become Professor of the Literature and Interpretation of the New Testament. A graduate of Harvard and of the School, he had been a tutor in Greek at the School in 1905–07, and had commuted from New York to give a course of lectures at the School in 1912. He held a Ph.D. from Harvard and a D.D. (earned, not honorary) from Union Seminary. During his ten years at General he had been developing that careful scholarship and encyclopedic knowledge which has made him the leading textual critic of the New Testament in America, and the author of a dozen authoritative books in his field. In a review of his recent *Principal Uncial Manuscripts of the New Testament*, Burton Scott Easton wrote: "For the magisterial character of the editing Dr. Hatch's name is an absolute guarantee; he stands unique among American — perhaps among living — scholars." For his book, *The Idea of Faith in Christian Literature*, the University of Strasbourg gave him a Th.D. and a cap and gown whose splendor would evoke the envy of a Greek Metropolitan.

The year that Hatch came was the year Fosbroke left. That year Gookin went into parish work, Muller went to China, Addison and Nash became chaplains in the army. In 1918 Washburn became Executive Secretary of the Church's War Commission. Had not the War engaged their attention, the Alumni might well have asked: "Where is the

---

[1] Among part-time teachers who served more than a year or two were J. C. Ayer, '87, Canon Law and Polity, 1900–05; C. A. Allen, Voice, 1901–08; W. A. Paul, Voice, 1908–17; R. G. Appel, Music, 1914–22, and 1925 to present. W. A. Paul enlivened his instruction by periodic recitals of the lyrics in Kipling's *Just So Stories* set to music by Edward German.

School we didn't know?" It almost ceased to exist. But of that later.

Meanwhile three new fields of study had been introduced into the curriculum: Sociology, the History of Religion and Missions, and Religious Pedagogy. Today we call the first Christian Social Ethics, the last Christian Education. In the first two the School was a pioneer.

As might have been expected from one so deeply concerned with the social responsibility of the Church, Hodges, immediately on his coming, introduced instruction in Sociology: he secured F. B. Allen of the Boston City Mission for a course of lectures. The next year, 1895, Robert Archey Woods, head of South End House, Boston, began his nineteen years of part-time teaching at the School. Hodges justly characterized him as "one of the most trusted leaders and one of the wisest counsellors of the present social movement." No other Episcopal Seminary was then or for some time after giving instruction in this subject. Only one seminary of any Church — the Chicago Theological Seminary — preceded the School, and that by but two years.

The School was likewise the first Episcopal seminary to establish a chair in the History of Religion and Missions.[2] This was in 1907. As early as 1878 Dr. Allen had given "An Introduction to the Study of Ethnic Religions," but discontinued it after 1890. In 1899 Dr. Edward Abbott gave a course on Missions in the Orient and James Haughton Woods, '90, of the Harvard Faculty, one on the History of Religion. He did so again in 1906. The next year Philip Mercer Rhinelander was called from the Berkeley Divinity School. Although not an authority in the field, he was an

[2] The chair was established by the efforts of the Alumni — see below, p. 152. H. B. Washburn, president of the Alumni Association, 1906–07, but not yet a member of the Faculty, consulted his friend, P. M. Rhinelander, about the proposed chair, and Rhinelander, without the least intimation that he might fill it, drafted the principles on which such a chair should be established. Later Washburn proposed Rhinelander's election.

enthusiastic student of it. His four years of teaching coincided with one of the School's peak periods of missionary interest. Just how much of this was due to him is difficult to estimate, for during portions of his time two Japanese students and one Chinese were in residence, as were the son and nephew of the School's first foreign missionary, Theodosius S. Tyng. There was also John Magee, who had been fired with missionary zeal before entering the School in 1908. In that year came the news of the death of E. H. Fitzgerald, '06, in China. All this would have produced some missionary fervor without Rhinelander, but he undoubtedly did much to encourage it. Of the men in the School during his time fifteen have spent some time in the foreign field. Even after deducting the three Oriental students, who in going to the "foreign field" simply went home, the number remains impressive. Fletcher Howe, Walworth Tyng, and John Magee, all of the class of 1911, have given practically life-long missionary service. Harry Beal, of the same class, is a missionary bishop.

The first lecturer in "Religious Pedagogy" was F. C. Lauderburn, vicar of St. Stephen's, Boston, in 1912. But this was by no means the first time the subject was taught at the School. The first Catalogue, we recall, expressed the hope if not the confidence that all the teachers were "pervaded by the true spirit of Sunday Schools." How far, if at all, this eventuated in any instruction in this field before 1894, it is impossible to say. It is certain that Dean Hodges from the beginning of his teaching included Sunday School and Confirmation instruction in his courses. There were few persons in the country better fitted to give it. He had conducted a large Sunday School in Pittsburgh; for ten years after coming to Cambridge he taught a weekly Bible Class for Sunday School teachers; he published Sunday School courses; his books for children were and still are masterpieces; all his lectures and sermons were models of instructional method. He was, in short, what today we would call a "natural" in the subject. When, however, the experts began to call it "Religious Pedagogy" the Dean modestly ceded the subject to others.

The introduction of new subjects naturally meant that room had to be found for them in the curriculum. A beginning in this direction had been made, as we recall, under Dean Lawrence, when Hebrew became optional after the first year. In 1903 it became optional in all years, and most men ceased to study it. A student might substitute elective courses offered in the School or courses in Harvard, if approved by the Faculty, and paid for by the student. Moreover, from this time on, for a decade, the better students were encouraged to take work at Harvard over and above their full theological schedule, and it became the recognized thing for an able man to take four additional Harvard courses during his theological course and thus earn an A.M. as well as a B.D. This ceased after 1913, when the University ruled that a student could not study for an A.M. while doing full work for another degree.

Meanwhile, by a rearrangement of the curriculum in 1909 a little more time was given for electives, and in 1914 required studies were so reduced that of the fourteen courses then needed for the degree, five were to be elective. This increase in the opportunity for elective study was coincident with the School's affiliation with Harvard, of which we shall speak later.

Possession of a bachelor's degree had been the requirement for admission to regular standing in the School since 1892. For admission as a special student two years of college work were required. In 1910 this was increased to three. A student so admitted might achieve regular standing by attaining an average of B in his first two years.

In 1905 the certificate (in use since 1879) was abandoned. Thereafter (until 1931) all students in regular standing who passed their course examinations satisfactorily and presented an acceptable thesis were to receive the B.D. Said the Dean: "The degree with us is just what it is at the law and medical schools. Every man who does his work reasonably well gets it." To make it the subject of special requirements is "inconsistent with general academic procedure." It was, however, decided that men whose marks were low were to be privately informed that they were awarded a "B.D. of the second grade." This quaint custom was only followed for a few years. In 1908 men whose work was of "distinguished excellence" received the degree *cum laude*, the rest, the degree without qualification.

Recommendations for the degree *honoris causa* were generously made by the Faculty from the earliest days of the School till the end of Hodges' deanship, and many who had received the certificate were given a B.D. after some years in the ministry, if they had proved their worth as parish priests.

In 1906 requirements for a D.D. were announced. They were modelled on those of Cambridge University. The candidate was to write a book which was to be assessed by a Reading Committee of scholars appointed by the Faculty but not of it. Concurrence of Committee, Faculty, and Trustees was necessary for the award of the degree, and the book was to be printed before the degree was conferred. Dr. Steenstra disapproved of the School's giving the degree at all. "The eagerness for degrees," he said, "is out of all proportion to their value." But the rest of the Faculty overruled him.

If a D.D., out of course, is to be given, the requirements here set forth go a long way toward making it respectable. It was offered, said the Dean, "for the purpose of encouraging productive scholarship among the clergy." Three degrees were awarded under these conditions: in 1907 to C. L. Slattery, '94, for his book *The Master of the World*; in

1910 to Frederic Palmer for *The Winning of Immortality*; and in 1913 to J. G. Hammarsköld, '88, for his translation of the Prayer Book into Swedish. That the degree was not lightly bestowed is evidenced by the refusal of it to other candidates (some of whom were to occupy positions of distinction not only in the Church but in the realm of scholarship) because their books were not judged to be of a sufficiently high quality.

The Faculty, however, was unable to abide by its own regulations and, in 1911, a D.D. was given on the ground that the recipient's work had been "the equivalent" of a book. In 1914 all reference to the D.D. was dropped from the catalogue. Since then sixteen more D.D.s have been given. Although it is not clear that any uniform standard has been applied in giving them, most of the recipients have been men of scholarly attainments. Owing to a divergence of opinion among the Faculty in recent years as to what the standard should be, no D.D. has been awarded since 1935.[3] Dean Washburn felt that the giving of honorary degrees by "a little institution like ours" was a "foolish practice" and should be wholly renounced.

[3] A master's degree in theology, representing a year's graduate study, was offered in 1912. Since 1936 it has been thought wise to leave the granting of this degree to the University.

XIV

AFFILIATION, FINANCES, AND THE WAR

WE RECALL how the University offered many of its facilities to the School at the time of its founding, how it described the School in the University Catalogue and in advertising copy in such a way as to lead many to suppose that it was a part of the University, how this troubled Dean Stone, and how Dean Gray had preferred to have it cease, lest it bring the School into theological disrepute. Friendly relations, however, between the two institutions continued, and the School's access to the Harvard libraries and museums was not interrupted. In 1900 the students of the School were admitted to the University's Gymnasium and in 1911 to its Infirmary.

The possibility of their taking courses at the University without additional cost was on Dean Hodges' mind from the time of his arrival in Cambridge. As early as May, 1894, he discussed it with Professor George Herbert Palmer. In 1901 he approached President Eliot informally with a proposal that University courses be opened to men at the School "without individual payment, on payment of a lump sum by our Trustees and on the opening of our courses to men of the University." President Eliot assured him that such a proposal, if formally made, "would be received with great cordiality." The Trustees of the School considered it, but took no action on it.

When the Andover Theological Seminary was about to move to Cambridge in 1908, Dean Hodges expressed the hope that Harvard, Andover, and the Episcopal School, might arrange for joint instruction in such subjects as sociology, religious education, and mental therapeutics.

As soon as Andover came to Cambridge it was affiliated with Harvard. The educational resources of each institution were open to the students of the other, yet each remained independent in organization and government, and each maintained its own faculty. In theory this offered a model for a possible affiliation of the School with Harvard, in practice it went much farther than the School was prepared to go, since the Harvard Divinity School moved in under the same roof with Andover in the new Andover Hall.

In 1911 Dean Fenn of the Harvard Divinity School told Dr. Kellner that he hoped that their respective Schools might be able to open certain courses to each other. In 1913, when Kirsopp Lake, then of Leyden, was to lecture at the School and the German scholar von Dobschütz at Harvard, the Univeristy made the suggestion that students of both institutions be admitted to these two courses without charge. To this the School readily assented.

It is not clear from whose side — Harvard's or the School's — the final impulse toward affiliation came, but in a conversation early in February, 1914, between Professor Washburn and Professor J. H. Ropes of the Harvard Divinity School, Ropes suggested that the best mode of approach would be a request from the School to the University "that the University should do something which you wanted done and would regard as a favor." Dean Hodges acted at once on Ropes' suggestion and asked President Lowell if they might confer on the subject. Meanwhile Ropes had talked to President Lowell and the President replied most cordially to the Dean.

As a result, President Lowell, Dean Fenn and Professor Foote of the Harvard Divinity School, Dean Hodges, and Professor Washburn met on February 16, 1914. At a subsequent meeting Bishop Lawrence, Mr. Dana, Professor

G. F. Moore of Harvard, and possibly some other Harvard representatives were also present, and early in March an agreement between Harvard and the School was drafted. After some slight revision, it was formally adopted by both institutions in May.

By the terms of this agreement the students of the School might take courses in the Divinity School or the Department of Arts and Sciences of the University without charge, such courses, if approved by the School's Faculty, to count toward the School's degree. Reciprocally, University students might, without charge, take courses in the School counting toward University degrees. A parallel arrangement was made with Andover.[1] The School was to raise its tuition from $50 to $150, making it equal to that of Andover and the Harvard Divinity School. Each institution might print in its catalogue a list of the courses in the others, and graduate students at the School might become candidates for the degrees of S.T.M. and S.T.D. at the University.

"The negotiations preliminary to this arrangement," said Dean Hodges, "have been characterized by a spirit of great generosity on the part of President Lowell and the University officials." Said President Lowell: "Both parties to the agreement feel that they have profited thereby. . . . The change benefits the whole body of students in both schools; and, in fact, any other profit to either school is of secondary moment. An institution of learning is a trustee, and no trustee should make for himself a profit from a bargain."

Since 1914 both the University Catalogue and the Bulletin of the Harvard Divinity School have regularly announced the courses of the School, and the School Catalogue

---

[1] Since the removal of Andover to Newton, distance has made its participation in the affiliation difficult, although the affiliation agreement is still maintained. A similar agreement with the Schools of Theology and of Religious Education in Boston University was entered into in 1921 and 1925 respectively.

has announced those of the Harvard Divinity School as well as a selection of other University courses. Moreover, as a matter of courtesy, the University has listed the professors of the School as members of the Harvard Faculty and accorded them all the privileges enjoyed by that body. Needless to say the School continues to manage its own affairs and is in no way subject to the control of the University. Its relation to Harvard has some similarity to the relation of an English college to an English university.

The opportunity which students in the School have been given of attending University courses, especially in philosophy, psychology, sociology, and education, has been a great gain. Nor has this advantage been wholly one-sided. University students, theological and otherwise, have, since the affiliation, regularly sat in the School's classes. Moreover, the School's Faculty has coöperated from time to time with the Harvard Theological Faculty in the joint conduct of courses attended by the students of both schools.

One result of the affiliation was the attendance at Dr. Kellner's classes of a number of Harvard undergraduates who desired to perfect themselves in their ancestral tongue. Thus it came about that Kellner taught Hebrew to the Hebrews! Dr. Taylor has more recently done the same.

Although both the School and the University were careful to make it clear in all their published statements that the affiliation was not a merger, and that the School maintained its separate existence, it seems that at least one person concluded from the affiliation, or possibly from the earlier statements which troubled Deans Stone and Gray, that the School had become an integral part of Harvard. By a will made in 1921 (and settled in 1939) Mrs. Marcella B. Upham left $150,000 "to the President and Fellows of Harvard College . . . the income thereof to be paid to the Episcopal Divinity School of Harvard College, to be used in assisting deserving students . . . the selection of those to whom aid shall be given to be determined by the Bishop of Massachusetts and the Dean of the said Divinity School."

The School felt that there could be little doubt as to the intention of the testator, but the University authorities maintained that since the bequest was made "to the President and Fellows of Harvard College," Harvard might rightfully claim it. In order to forestall a law suit and the possible loss of the money by both the School and Harvard to a residuary legatee, a compromise was effected by which the School received $100,000, Harvard $50,000.

As has been noted, the affiliation agreement called for an increase of the School's tuition to that charged at the Harvard Divinity School, for if the advantages of both schools were open to students in either, the school with the lower tuition might enroll all the students. But for an Episcopal seminary to charge $150 tuition, or indeed to charge any tuition, was unprecedented except in Cambridge. Here a charge of $50 a year had been made since 1896. Two years before, Dean Hodges had said: "It is easier financially for a young man to enter Holy Orders than to do almost anything else . . . a tuition fee would operate to hinder men from coming lightly and unadvisedly into the ministry." For those who could not possibly pay the fee, whether $50 or $150, scholarship aid was given in the form of payment for work done in churches and Sunday Schools which could not themselves pay for it.

Hodges, like his predecessors, lamented the School's small scholarship endowment. To this Mr. Lincoln of the Trustees added $15,000. This, plus annual gifts from the Chapel congregation and other friends, enabled the Dean to print in the Catalogue that "no man whose character and ability give promise of a useful ministry" need "be deterred by financial reasons from entering the School." It was not always easy for him to make good this promise, for living expenses in Cambridge were high — higher than in any other Episcopal seminary. In 1916 the estimated minimum for the school year (including only tuition, room rent, board, and light) was $400. In 1894 it had been $250; in 1919 it was $525.[2] Board in the refectory had, by occasional subsidy from the Trustees, been kept at $4.25 a week from 1880 to 1902. Then began a gradual increase. In 1908 it was $5.00; in 1917, $6.00.

These figures, frankly printed in the Catalogue, doubtless frightened away some prospective students, and the fact that work was connected with scholarship aid, while in other seminaries aid was often given unconditionally, probably proved an additional deterrent, though perhaps a wholesome one. Said the Dean: "The young man who intends to study for the ministry should meet the same test which confronts the young man who undertakes a course of preparation for the law or medicine, the test of difficulty." "Side by side with a great school of medicine and a great school of law, the school of theology stands on the same basis of self respect. It does not offer free education."[3]

When the five year pledges, secured by the Trustees at Dean Hodges' coming, ran out in 1899, the Dean asked Mr. Amory "to take the Blue Book and go through it systematically, marking the name of every person who might possibly be disposed to give us at least $100 a year." The Dean then wrote personal notes to these persons. On the reverse

[2] These minimum fixed charges rose to $560 in 1920, came down to $500 in 1932, and since 1935 have been $400. A charge for fuel was made in 1877, one for care of room in 1878 (called room rent in 1901); combined into a $55 room rent in 1904; abolished in 1935.

[3] Bishop Lawrence later pointed out that while this observation of Dean Hodges about law and medicine holds good for regions where there are privately endowed universities, a large part of the country, where there are state universities, does offer free education in law and medicine without undermining the self-respect of the students. The latter practice, he said, is essentially American and ought to be made possible for theological schools by endowment for scholarships.

of the notepaper there was printed a statement of the School's needs. In this and other ways between twelve and fourteen thousand dollars a year was raised until 1904.

Meanwhile in 1900 Mr. William C. Schermerhorn of New York, whose interest in the School had been awakened by William Reed Huntington, offered $25,000 toward the endowment of a professorship, provided $75,000 more was secured. The Trustees, after raising $25,000 in special gifts, allocated $50,000 from the School's capital funds to make up the balance. The Professorship of Homiletics and Pastoral Theology thus endowed was named for Dean Stone. It was the School's first endowed professorship and was thereafter held by Dean Hodges.

The Dean's attention to the salaries of the professors did not cease with the increases which they received at his coming. Early in 1902 he appealed to the Trustees again. "The condition of the health of Mr. Nash and Mr. Drown," he wrote, "is the immediate reason for my concern in this matter. Mr. Nash is already the leading New Testament scholar of our Church, not to say of our country. His learning is unusually great, and his ability as a writer and a teacher keeps pace with it. But Mr. Nash is obliged to give two days and a half of every week to the care of a parish at Chestnut Hill. He is obliged to do this on account of the smallness of his salary. This double burden is not only depriving us of so much of his time, but is undoubtedly shortening his life." He went on to say that Drown, also because of inadequate salary, had been obliged to teach two days a week at Wellesley. "No man can serve this School aright who gives that amount of time to outside work unless he kills himself: a process in which both of these men are engaged. Moreover, if Mr. Kellner stays in the School at his present stipend he is compelled to celibacy. This is a sacrifice which we have no right to ask. Mr. Kellner is the best Hebrew teacher in the country. We could not adequately fill his place." He asked that the salaries of Steenstra, Allen, and Nash be made $3,000, those of Drown and Kellner $2,500; and he offered to raise the $4,000 a year needed for this if the Trustees would sanction the increases. They did.

The Dean proceeded to raise the money by securing contributions from about fifteen alumni, a few laymen, and half a dozen parishes where he preached about the School. He did not have to continue this for more than a year, for in March, 1904, the widow of Benjamin Tyler Reed died. Mr. Reed's son's widow, who was still living, had a life interest in a third of the estate, but two-thirds of it, amounting to about $330,000, now came to the School.

The Dean and Trustees hastened to issue a statement to all the friends of the School apprising them of this and thanking them for their past support. "Except for your generosity," they said, "the School could not have lived." In the past year they had given $14,000. The income to be expected from the newly acquired Reed money was $15,-000. Thus, without any more annual contributions, the School could go on as it had been going. But it could not advance. Hence the hope was expressed that those who had given in the past would do so in the future. Scholarships and fellowships [4] and instructorships were needed, as were additional funds for books and a library building.

As a result of this and subsequent appeals, about $9,000 came in annually; $20,000 was left by the Rev. Edmund T.

---

[4] The Dean's oft-made plea for graduate fellowships was answered by occasional gifts. The first was from C. J. Blake for a fellowship in Sociology in 1904. Subsequent fellowship donors were G. F. Peabody in 1905; Mrs. Allen (now Mrs. Drown) in 1912, in memory of Dr. Allen; Mrs. G. L. Cheney in 1913. From 1924 to 1929, the Trustees made annual fellowship appropriations. The "Friends' Fund" has provided fellowships since 1930. Four fellowship holders have subsequently served on the School's Faculty, one at the Virginia Seminary, and one at St. John's University, Shanghai. There is as yet no fellowship endowment.

Slafter, the income of which was to buy books; a new library building, costing $35,000, was built; and the Alumni undertook to endow a professorship.

The library was the gift of John Gordon Wright, a friend and parishioner of Dr. Nash in Chestnut Hill, and a Trustee of the School from 1908 till his death in 1912. In that year the library was completed. He had been convinced that the School needed it by Dr. Kellner. The room in Reed Hall which had hitherto housed the library was then remodelled as a lecture hall by G. L. Paine. '00, in memory of his father, Robert Treat Paine.

Although the library was the most considerable expansion in physical equipment in Dean Hodges' time, it was not the only one. A house for Dr. Drown (12 Phillips Place) was built in 1902; the School grounds were rounded out by the purchase in 1907 of the house and land at 6 Phillips Place, which became the home of Dr. Nash; [5] a new Chapel organ was installed in 1900; in 1904 a single heating plant replaced the twelve previously used; in 1899 gas fixtures were put in Lawrence Hall; in 1900 a telephone. By 1913 electricity was in most of the buildings, but it did not reach Lawrence Hall till 1922.

What seems to have been the first effort of the Alumni, as an association, to raise money was in 1895, when they set out to support one of their number in the mission field. L. H. Roots, '96, was so supported until his consecration as Bishop of Hankow in 1904; then three more missionaries to China, E. H. Fitzgerald, '06, till his early death in 1908; Dudley Tyng, '09, till 1916; and Walworth Tyng, '11, till 1936. Since then the contributions have been divided between two or three different missionary alumni each year.

In 1901 a "Committee on the Larger Powers of the Alumni," consisting of A. H. Amory, '80, E. S. Rous-

[5] Subsequently occupied by Professors Gookin, Norman Nash, Taylor, and Johnson.

maniere, '86, and J. W. Suter, '85, of which Suter appears to have been the leading spirit, addressed the Trustees. The Alumni, they said, should be utilized for the strengthening of the School by bringing them into "some closer relation to its affairs." They might, for instance, be asked to elect representatives who should exercise functions "similar to those exercised by the Board of Overseers of Harvard College"; and if they knew more about the School's finances they might help with them.

A committee of the Trustees thereupon met with the Alumni Committee, the Bishop, and the Dean, and it was decided that the Alumni should elect a "Board of Alumni Associates," who would meet twice a year with the Trustees to confer on the welfare of the School. A board of six was elected (called "Executive Committee" after 1908); they first met with the Trustees in 1902 and regularly thereafter for twenty years. It was also in 1902 that Cambridge Clubs were organized in New York and Rhode Island, for mutual stimulus, and for "any good they may be able to render the School."

We find this entry in the Dean's diary for January 28, 1904: "This evening dinner of the Cambridge Club of New York at the Arena, a queer place. Dr. Steenstra having spoken for three quarters of an hour, I came away to get the midnight train, leaving half a dozen speakers still expectant."

Later the same year the Dean, when presenting the wants of the School to the parish of an alumnus, said: "The salaries are small, but within a few years one professor has declined a parochial offer of $6,000, and another of $8,000. That sort of devotion invites a response and gets it." The allusion was to a call to himself to return to Calvary, Pittsburgh, in 1899, and to one from Holy Trinity, Brooklyn, to Dr. Nash in 1903. A year later the Dean declined a call to Leland Stanford University at a salary of $10,000.

In 1905 the Alumni Associates decided that it was time

for action and, at the suggestion of the Dean and the Trustees, proposed to the Alumni the endowment of a chair in the History of Religion and Missions. At the June meeting in 1906 the Alumni voted to raise $75,000 for this in three years. The Alumni were over sanguine. They were to discover that it is easier for a group gathered at Commencement enthusiastically to vote that the Alumni body as a whole — two-thirds of which may not be present — will raise $75,000 than to raise it. The depression of 1907 discouraged giving. The resignation of Rhinelander in 1911 doubtless added to the discouragement. But that was two years after the $75,000 was supposed to have been raised. At that time $12,500 had been collected. In 1922, sixteen years after the original resolution, the fund had reached but $20,000.

In 1912 Trustees and Alumni launched another campaign, this time for a $500,000 endowment. But another depression, in 1913, killed it after $9,000 had come in.

In 1916 the Alumni Committee on the School's fiftieth anniversary, to be celebrated at Commencement, 1917, proposed still another drive for $500,000. The international situation cast a damper on this and J. W. Suter, who continued to be the somewhat over-hopeful leader in these projects, found it impossible to get even the members of the Trustee-Alumni Endowment Committee to meet.

"I hope you can enlist the Bishop," wrote E. T. Sullivan, '92, to Suter, "He is wise to the point of genius." Whether Suter tried to do so is not clear, but Dr. Kellner, roused by the inaction of both Trustees and Alumni, took matters into his own hands, although he was not a member of the Committee. He got in touch with Bishop Lawrence and together they rounded up not only the Committee but several other leading alumni, who elected the Bishop honorary chairman of the campaign and prepared for action. The entry of America into the war made postponement imperative, but the enlistment of the Bishop was, as it proved later, the significant outcome of the movement.

Despite the war, the fiftieth anniversary was celebrated with due festivity. Some hundred and sixty alumni attended the dinner on the night before Commencement and, at the Commencement exercises, marched in procession, vested, together with the representatives of other institutions. At the end of the procession came Bishop Lawrence and President Lowell.

At the Alumni dinner there was much reminiscing about the early days of the School and its former teachers. This, said Dean Hodges, recalled "the formula of the tragedy of professional life, which is that after a sufficient number of years have passed all that is remembered of us is our eccentricities. We do not seem to be so eccentric as our predecessors were; but what goes on in the undergraduate mind nobody can tell."

Although the war had not prevented the celebration of the School's fiftieth anniversary, it rapidly depleted the School itself. The student body dropped from fifty in 1914–15 to seventeen in 1917–18, and to eight in the fall of 1918. There were then four seniors, one middler, and three special students, one of whom was a Chinese and one a Greek. There were no juniors. The United States Naval Radio School rented all of the School buildings except the library and the Chapel. The School in turn rented No. 10 Mason Street, one of the little brick houses across from the deanery, for a student dormitory. Classes were held in the library. The resident Faculty consisted of the Dean, Kellner, and Drown. Washburn, as Executive Secretary of the Church's War Commission, had to spend most of his time in New York, and Hatch came up two days a week from Providence, where he was in charge of St. Martin's, while its rector was serving as a Red Cross chaplain.

In March, 1917, the Faculty voted that a student who

entered "any form of national service" would be given a full year's credit on the basis of marks already recorded. Although all seniors finished their course, twelve undergraduates entered war service, nine of them in the armed forces, two in the Y.M.C.A., and one as an ambulance driver at the front.

Over fifty of the Alumni, including Instructors Addison and Nash, were also in war service, mostly as chaplains and Y.M.C.A. workers overseas and voluntary chaplains at camps in this country; four were in the armed forces. H. R. Talbot, '98, L. Rollins, '12, and W. E. Patrick, '15, chaplains, and M. J. Barker, Jr., '16, of the Y.M.C.A., were decorated for bravery, as were two of the undergraduates, H. W. Hobson, '20, and H. I. Fair, '21, both of whom were twice wounded in action. Ambulance driver C. C. Jatho, '18, spent six months in a German prison.

In January, 1919, seven former students came back from war service, and four new men entered. For them and others who followed them an opportunity to make up nearly a year of their preparation was provided in two sessions of a summer school at Middletown, Connecticut, in 1919 and 1920, supported jointly by the Philadelphia, General, Berkeley, and Cambridge Schools. Drown and Hatch represented Cambridge on its faculty in 1919, Hatch and Nash in 1920.

January, 1919, marked the completion of Dean Hodges' twenty-fifth year at the School. He had been seriously ill in 1915; after a year in California he had returned in apparently good health and excellent spirits, but in the fall of 1918 there were premonitions of another break, and he had to go slowly. He was heartened by the recognition accorded his twenty-five years of service in Cambridge. At a reception in January, 1919, the Chapel congregation gave him a purse of $2,500, and at the mid-winter Alumni dinner in February there was a silver bowl filled with gold coins.

What cheered him most was the outpouring of devotion which accompanied it. "One wonders," said Dr. Kellner, "whether there was ever such a collective expression of personal affection before."

The Dean went on with his work, but renewed heart symptoms in March compelled him to stop. "I have been off my job for two weeks with shortness of breath," he wrote cheerfully to a friend on the 31st. "I am accustomed to shortness of ideas, but this new difficulty troubles me. The remedy is rest, to be taken every day between meals." He went to his summer home at Holderness, New Hampshire, where he died on May 27.

XV

HENRY SYLVESTER NASH

Henry Sylvester Nash, son of a country parson, was born in Newark, Ohio, in 1854. His boyhood was spent in country parishes in Illinois, Kentucky, Nebraska, and Iowa. His going to college was delayed for two years beyond the usual age by the necessity of earning money to go. From Mt. Sterling, Iowa, he came to Harvard in June, 1875, obtained a list of reading for the freshman year, passed an examination on it at the end of the summer, and was admitted as a sophomore. He graduated in 1878 with the reputation of having taken more books out of the college library than any other man who had ever attended Harvard. He read rapidly; his phenomenal memory enabled him to retain what he read.

He entered the Theological School in 1878 and graduated in 1881, although he attended classes during his junior and senior years only. The work of his middle year he took by reading and examination while teaching at a boys' school. Dr. Allen, at the Theological School's fortieth anniversary, said there had never been another student in the School as brilliant as Nash.

In 1882, after a year's graduate study, Nash became an instructor; the next year, at the age of twenty-nine, a full professor. Said Dean Gray, "He was born and raised up for this work, in the opinion of us all." "He has the modesty of the true scholar," said Dr. Steenstra, "who never ceases to be a learner."

A description of Nash's teaching has been left us by C. L. Slattery, '94, who studied with him a decade after he began to teach: "He spent the first year in a rapid reading of the Greek Testament, with introductions to the various books, and special consideration of the Synoptic problem and the sources of the life of Christ; the second year we worked over the Epistle to the Romans in minute detail; the third year was devoted to the Fourth Gospel.

"In the first year he threw us up against the most difficult critical questions of the age. We wrote nine theses that first year. The first was on the Tübingen Hypothesis — of which till then none of us had ever heard. We then wrote a thesis based upon a reading of the New Testament to find every reference and allusion to the Parousia. He commanded us to read many Lives of Christ and required us to relate in a thesis the point of view and method of each. Some men were frightened by the robustness of the attack. We were given the supreme documents of Christianity; if they were filled with hard questions which might later unsettle our faith, we were forced to face the issue at once. Dr. Nash treated us on the first day of the course as grown men.

"However, in meeting whatever difficulties there were, we had the superb help of Dr. Nash's own faith. He never dodged the perplexities. Some critical questions he felt to be settled. Others he held in solution. Still others he believed insoluble in this world. Once when a pupil asked him what St. Paul meant by a certain phrase, he said with a reverence which was from the heart, 'I don't know; that is one of the questions I mean to ask St. Paul when I see him.'

"Nash was at his height in his exposition of the Epistle to the Romans. He struggled to give us all that commentators in the past had thought; then he gave us his own interpretation; and beyond that, he gave us the profound expression of his own faith. Then it was that we would look up from our note books — in which we had been writing furiously to get every word down — to discover that the face of our teacher, once thought exceedingly plain, was radiantly beautiful, shining as the face of an angel. We knew that the Holy Ghost was upon him."

This radiance which at times lit up Nash's face was remarked by many who heard him in class room or pulpit. Said Dr. Drown, who used to aver, with undue modesty, that all the theology he knew he had learned from Nash, "The face of Henry Nash was a transfigured face. When we fastened our eyes on him in prayer, in preaching, in meditation, in sacred fellowship, we saw his face illumined. The homely features were transfigured in the light of the eternal. Like Moses he had seen God on the height, and his face shone."

H. C. Robbins, '03, who was in the School ten years after Slattery, spoke of Nash's scholarship as "suffused with a profound spirituality, which made him the most influential person in the School." D. M. Brookman, '00, when enlightening the people of Christ Church, Dayton, Ohio, about the School in 1904, spoke of the Faculty in somewhat lighter vein. "Dr. Nash," he said, "in appearance reminds some people of Robert Louis Stevenson. He talks in parables and strange phrases, and is said to read two books in bed every night before falling asleep."

"Parables and strange phrases" was not a misstatement. Slattery admits that Nash "used a language which was no one's but his own. Even the illustrations — which were apt to be very odd indeed, sometimes grotesque — were mystifying." This grotesqueness was celebrated in the not too respectful faculty song, perpetrated by J. F. Scott and G. E. Norton of the class of 1910:

> Here's to Henry Sylvester Nash
> Who feeds us exegetical hash,
> He turns our stomachs more than a little
> By calling Agrippa "an old lick-spittle."

Roland Cotton Smith, '85, said he once sent a servant girl

for his Greek Testament, describing it as the only book on his desk which she could not read. She returned with Nash's *Genesis of the Social Conscience*.

This obscurity of style was a cross to Nash. He struggled to overcome it and to a considerable extent succeeded in the last and perhaps greatest of his four published books, *The Atoning Life*.

The Genesis of the Social Conscience is, in its very title, an indication of one of Nash's prime concerns. As Dean Hodges said in 1917, "The social leadership which is shown by so many of our Alumni, and which has made them so conspicuously useful in the communities to which they minister, is largely due to the personal influence of Dr. Nash." We have already noted his creation of the "My Neighbor Club" for the study of the Church's social responsibility, and his leadership of it for thirteen years.

"He was," said Slattery, "religiously democratic. He would sometimes remind us that our Lord was accustomed to be with the sort of people who in our time eat with their knives. He had a beautiful chivalry in the presence of servants. Without departing from any conventionality he would by a glance, a smile, or the slightest of words, acknowledge even at another's table the acts of service by which he was surrounded. He was a great gentleman, who made many other gentlemen look quite cheap."

Said Nash himself, "The function of a true gentleman is to open up to those he meets new sources of self-respect within themselves."

My Class in the School was one of the last to sit under Nash. One member of it thought then and still thinks that Nash was worth all the rest of the Faculty rolled into one. I myself and, I believe, most of my classmates, found Nash often beyond us. Although we got much from him, we got more from less verbally obscure and perhaps less learned members of the Faculty.

Dean Hodges, after hearing Nash speak at a summer school, wrote in his journal: "Nash's lecture fairly coruscated with epigrams and fine thoughts but was a bit over my head."

Dr. Drown, in his sermon at the time of Nash's death, spoke of Nash's loneliness, his fighting his own fights within his own soul. "In trouble and under pressure," wrote Nash, "*burn your own smoke.*" "Perhaps," added Drown, "he did that too much. . . . And then too there was his commanding intellect. Perhaps it was inevitable that we his friends stood more or less in awe of him."

Certainly we students stood more or less in awe of him — mostly more. But it was not his intention that we should. In his note books he admonished himself thus: "Your danger as a teacher is the forgetting that your men can and must teach you." "Are you patient enough in learning what your men think? Are you not too hot to tell them what you think?" "Learn to be glad when one of your men picks a flaw in your work."

The trouble with us was that we didn't know enough to pick a flaw in his work, had we dared.

Dr. Drown used to tell how he once asked Nash whether he thought that if he (Drown) went to Germany for a year he could learn to read German as readily as he read English, "Yes," said Nash, "you could. But you don't need to go to Germany. You can do it here. Why not? You can do it with Greek, why not with German?" "To us lesser men," said Drown, "this seemed a curious argument."

"If," wrote Nash in exhortation to himself in one of his note books, "your desire to know the Hebrew Bible ever flags, let the thought, 'This was my Lord's mental food,' stir you like a trumpet." He read Hebrew, Greek, Latin, French, and German as he read English, and late in life learned Italian.

Despite his awesome learning and his occasional obscu-

rity in expression, there were frequent flashes in his teaching
of sublime lucidity. I recall his discussion of Justification by
Faith. God's belief in us, he said, is like our friend's belief
in us: it makes us humble and it makes us strong. We accept
God's belief in us, God's estimate of us, just as we accept
our mother's, our sweetheart's, our friend's — on faith. We
know ourselves to be unworthy of it, but our acceptance
of it is a source of strength, enabling us in some small measure to live up to it. Thus when we believe that God believes
in us, there comes a new power into our lives making for
righteousness; we are justified, made righteous, by faith —
by our faith in God's faith in us. That was the center of
Nash's theology. He felt it was the center of St. Paul's.
Perhaps it is the center of all truly Christian theology.

If Nash was obscure in his books, he was less so in his
classroom, and still less in the pulpit, while in his prayers he
achieved a simplicity and a clarity which have won them a
lasting place in the literature of devotion. They give us a
glimpse into the consecration and sanctity of his own character:

"O God, our great companion, lead us day by day deeper
into the mystery of life, and make us interpreters of life to
our fellows."

"Bless us, dear God, with the vision of thy being and
beauty, that in the strength of it we may work without haste
and without rest."

"Master of life, lead us through patient study and un-
wearying prayer into the deeper knowledge of thee."

"Illumine our minds with the light of thine own reason,
inform our wills with thine eternal purpose, and so make
our daily work a prayer."

He was called to the Church of the Holy Trinity, Brooklyn, at more than twice his Cambridge salary. He was
offered a chair in philosophy at the University of Michigan.

He was asked to let himself be nominated for the bishopric of Rhode Island and assured that if he did so his election would be practically certain. All these offers he declined.

His devotion to the School grew not only out of his almost life-long association with it, but also and chiefly out of his profound sense of its spiritual mission. This he grandly expressed on the death, in 1904, of his friend Augustine Heard Amory, '80: "I joined with him year after year in the Quiet Day at the Theological School, when the Alumni come back there to refresh themselves in the memories of that blessed place — that blessed place, where doubt and study and disillusionment and consecration all together blended in them to fire them with a zeal for the honor of God."

Nash was not physically strong and he overworked. In 1900–01 he had a long severe illness, from which he never wholly recovered. In 1907 it was diagnosed as Hodgkin's disease, for which there is no cure. In 1908 it was found that his second son, then a senior at Harvard, in whom he greatly delighted, had diabetes. That was before the discovery of insulin. I have only recently learned these facts. From 1908 to 1910 I sat in Nash's classes; I frequently visited his home; neither I nor, so far as I know, any of my school-mates saw in him the least sign that he was living under this double sentence of death. Now the words of one of his great prayers take on a new meaning:

"O God, author of the world's joy, bearer of the world's pain, make us glad that we have inherited the world's burden; deliver us from the luxury of cheap melancholy; and, at the heart of all our trouble and sorrow, let unconquerable gladness dwell."

When his *Atoning Life* was published, a reviewer in *The Boston Herald* wrote: "A man who lives his teachings stands back of the book, and we read it with the thought of the simplicity that makes goodness a natural thing, and the bright courage that faces pain and danger even more bravely than Stevenson did, because more quietly."

On March 6, 1912, at the age of fifty-eight, Nash died. He had served the School thirty years.

"He impressed upon us as no other man we ever met," said J. H. Melish, '98, "the sanctity of reason and the majesty of prayer."

XVI

HENRY BRADFORD WASHBURN

IN SEPTEMBER, 1919, the Faculty united to recommend to the Trustees Charles Lewis Slattery, '94, rector of Grace Church, New York, as Dean. Although the Trustees were under no obligation to accept this recommendation, they gladly did so and elected him. He declined, but within a few years came into intimate touch with the School as Bishop of Massachusetts.

In January, 1920, the Trustees elected Henry Bradford Washburn, also of the class of '94. Born in Worcester, Massachusetts, in 1869, he had graduated from Harvard in 1891 and, after three years at the School, studied for two in Berlin and Oxford. He was chosen, at Dr. Allen's suggestion, to teach Church History in the School during Allen's sabbatical in 1901–02. Meanwhile he was gaining parochial experience, first as assistant for two years at St. John's, Providence, and after that as rector of St. Mark's, Worcester, for ten. On Allen's death in 1908 he was elected to the chair of Church History in the School. This was perhaps the most difficult position which any man in the history of the School has been called upon to fill, for the Alumni, every one of whom had sat under Allen, felt that no one could possibly fill Allen's place.

Thirty-two years later one of Allen's most enthusiastic disciples, J. W. Suter, '85, who as a member of the Board of Visitors had sat in Washburn's classes as well as listened to his periodic lectures to the Alumni, said, "Allen in his inspiring way philosophized and theologized Church History, Washburn has vivified and humanized it."

Washburn came more and more to feel that the key to Church History was Christian biography, that the religious experience of the leaders of the Church was "the stuff out of which institutions and doctrines were made"; and his courses in biography were among the most rewarding and the most popular in the School. They remained so up to the last day of his teaching in 1940. His two published volumes are illustrations of the masterly way in which he could sum up in brief space the facts and the meaning of a man's career and estimate his abiding significance. They are also illustrations of the catholicity of his interests, for, as he says in the introduction to *Men of Conviction*, "not one of them is a Protestant Episcopalian, not even Athanasius!"

What impressed his students was the fairness with which he presented views opposed to his own and the charity with which he judged the motives of those who stood for everything which he did not. As one alumnus put it, he learned from him not only Church History but courtesy: "By courtesy I understood him to mean such things as presenting views which he did not like as well as he knew how to present them, and not making grotesque straw men who can so easily be knocked down." Another has said that he learned from him "the art of appreciation" — genuine appreciation of others' beliefs and practices instead of "smug tolerance" of them. He was, said still another, "calm and unperturbed, open-minded, ideally fair and just, bound to hear both sides with equal patience and consideration, to penetrate if possible to the real point of truth underlying the question at issue."

His judicial appraisal of opposite estimates of a character and of both sides of a historic (or a contemporary) controversy and his endeavor to grasp the truth in each, was celebrated in verse at one of the Christmas plays:

> Professor Washburn "likes to think"
> That there are theories three.
> The third combines the other two
> Throughout Church Hist-or-ie.

What weighed with many of his students quite as much as his vivid and generous portrayal of the saints and sinners of the past was the reflection in his own character of the virtues which he discovered in them. Many a graduate has borne testimony to this. The following, from John Crocker, '30, is typical: "It is not merely that he introduced us to a succession of great figures. It is rather that their example struck home with peculiar force, because the rock-hewn strength of their lives was, we knew, concretely reflected in his own. He made us see that what these men were in former times a man could be to-day."

If the filling of Allen's place had been difficult, the filling of Dean Hodges' was no less so. More than one alumnus expressed uncertainty about Washburn's capacity to fill it. But when, in 1940, H. C. Robbins, '03, wrote to him, "You have become for us in a very real sense an embodiment of the spirit of the School," he undoubtedly voiced the sentiment of the two hundred and fifty living graduates of Dean Hodges' time.

At the Alumni dinner in St. Louis in 1916, when, as we have seen, the Alumni discussed the parlous state of the School, J. W. Suter, '85, had raised two questions. To these Washburn wrote a reply. It was a forecast of his attitude as Dean:

"Your questions at St. Louis — what is the School going to stand for? what is it going to do under the conditions created by the affiliation with the University? — are questions that are constantly on our minds. I hardly see how an immediate answer can be made to either. The answers must come through the gradual adaptation of our teaching and of our curriculum to the needs of the present. We are in a position totally different from that of Allen, Steenstra, and the others fifty years ago. . . . Their work is now done. Schools that suspected their contribution now take it for granted. . . . We take our stand fearlessly on the ground that these men occupied: we believe unfalteringly both in scholarship and in adapting the training of the men to the needs of the day; we do not believe in tradition merely because it is tradition. . . . I am confident that we need primarily spiritual leadership, and that this must be accompanied by a curriculum so elastic that men of pronounced desire and ability to specialize may do so. I am also confident that the Protestantism for which we stand is going to be a very much more inclusive Protestantism than that for which your teachers and mine stood. . . . Something infinitely more conserving of the wide exprience of the Church in all its branches we must have."

In his inaugural address he said that the primary task of the School was the maintenance of "an inner life of a very high order." The essentials for this were "sound scholarship," "a practical purpose," and "a simple, vital religion." "No teacher," he said, "should be added to the staff unless he show promise of becoming a scholar." But "scholarship must have a goal beyond itself." The Faculty "should be individually and collectively controlled by the pastoral instinct." Moreover, "scholarship, together with its practical purpose, should be altogether under the control of religion." "Young men training for the ministry want religion before anything else." The Faculty "must look upon religion as their primary concern. . . . We must try very hard to be Christians in our homes, . . . in our communities, . . . in our class rooms — patient, just, personally concerned in the student, as deeply interested in the man of limited intelli-

gence as in his more brilliant classmate; we must try to be
Christians with one another, recognizing our fellowship in
a common task."

Difficult as the attainment of this ideal may have been for
some of the Faculty, there is no question that Dean Washburn exemplified it himself. His justice, his patience, his
concern for the individual student, his interest in the man of
limited intelligence were proverbial. If he discerned real
promise for the ministry in a student who had not the ghost
of a chance to pass the School's examinations, he would
spend months coaching him for his canonicals.

The first impression he made on many a new man was that
of austere reserve, even severity. A neighbor of the School
spoke of him as "the last Puritan." "His keen look — the
whole man — condemned the superfluous," said an alumnus
recently. "Strong in moral perception and integrity," was
the way another described him. Bishop Lawrence characterized him as "a typical New Englander," but added "of
the best sort" — one behind whose "outward, formal, and at
times severe mien, which is truly of New England," lay "a
sense of humor, dry and stimulating, and a warmth of friend-
liness and charity, characteristic of only the choicest of New
England."

If the students' first impression was of his "severe mien,"
it was soon modified when, on a visit to his home, they
found him on his hands and knees on the floor, covered with
a bear-skin rug, playing bear hunt with his two small sons,
or, by an astonishing combination of suppleness of limb and
ramrod erectness of body, giving an imitation, behind the
sofa, of a man going down the cellar and coming up again
with a jug of cider. Nor did it take long to learn, as one
of them said, that "his strictness with himself became the
gentlest of consideration in his dealings with us." His "patience with the learning mind," "his thoughtful guiding of

our thinking, never forced, always gently counselled," is what the graduates remember.

"While you gave us much in the lives of others," wrote Benedict Williams, '30, to him at the time of his retirement, referring to his courses in biography, "you gave us more by your own life. While we could set our watches by your time schedule and our lives by your strict self-discipline, you didn't expect it of us, and were willing with unfailing courtesy to overlook our failures. Because you drew the picture without asking for copies, we are inclined as the years go on to pattern our lives after the picture."

A discerning undergraduate in the class of 1928 once said to a classmate, "I think Dean Washburn makes this resolution every morning: 'Today I am going to be a Christian.'"

In addition to his work as Dean and teacher of Church History, he frequently gave courses in preaching and pastoral care, and by both precept and example in these fields — perhaps most by example — moulded the men.

"Without moving a muscle he stood on the chancel steps," said G. R. Metcalf, '32, "pouring forth precise, crystal-clear phrases. This physical immobility gave his words a compelling power we have not found in any other speaker. And what consolation it gave us to learn from his own lips that such ease of speech resulted from years of conscious study and unceasing practice." "He made me abhor cheap expressions, slang, vulgarity, such things as debased language," said W. L. Beckwith, '16, "and inspired me to say what I have to say simply and reverently." Many have spoken of his "superb understanding of words and their precise value."

"You reminded us," wrote A. P. Stokes, Jr., '32, to him in 1940, "by your clear-cut definitions that breadth of mind does not mean sloppiness of mind. Even the tidiness of your dress (accentuated by your habit of smoothing out your waistcoat — one of your little mannerisms we liked to mimic) has reminded us that if we are to be effective parsons we must live continuously 'decently and in order.' "

"One word more, gentlemen," the Dean would say at the end of his yearly address of welcome to the new men, "Your clothes may not always be new, but your general appearance can always be worthy of your profession. A can of shoe polish costs only ten cents."

"There is undeniable versatility in a teacher's offering," said R. E. Maxwell, '35, "when his disciples are made to think of him every time they look for the good in Hildebrand as well as every time they polish their shoes."

In one of the years when he was away on a sabbatical, the Faculty took the opportunity to express to the Trustees their appreciation of him as Dean: "He has shown marked executive ability and has planned in a far-sighted manner for the future of the School. In his relations with the Faculty he has been eminently fair-minded and has welcomed all differences of opinion as contributions to the common good." "We have worked together in great harmony."

It is this "great harmony" in the Faculty which has been the joy and amazement of those who have joined it after experience at other institutions. It has been characteristic of the School from its earliest days; but that it has been conserved and increased is not the least of Dean Washburn's contributions to the School's life.

On his retirement in 1940, he was presented with a "Book of Remembrance" in which letters from 420 alumni were bound. "Many things are said in it," wrote the Dean, "that I can hardly believe. Nevertheless they make comforting reading . . . and in every letter, whatever its dominant note, is the tender and vigorous declaration that for all these years we have been members of a large, congenial, and happy family."

Although the alumni family has not always been large, it

has, from the beginning, been singularly congenial and happy. That it has continued to be so, despite its increasing size, is in a marked degree Dean Washburn's achievement. In this Mrs. Washburn has shared. Her bountiful hospitality has made the deanery a place to which an alumnus returns as naturally as to his own home.

XVII

DEAN WASHBURN FACES THE FUTURE

WHEN Washburn became dean many of the alumni were saying that the Church and the School were passing through a crisis. He reminded them that he had learned from his study of history that the Church's "normal experience has been that of crisis," and he proposed to face the future "indifferent to the persuasions of the discouraged."

One phase of the crisis through which the Church was passing was a resurgence of Fundamentalism. In November, 1923, the Bishops met at Dallas, Texas. Less than half of them (sixty-five out of one hundred and forty-four) were present. Those who were issued a Pastoral Letter for the "guidance" of the Church on the subject of the creeds, and especially on the clause in the Apostles' Creed concerning the Virgin Birth. Any other than a literal interpretation of this, they said, was dishonest and, in a clergyman, irreconcilable with his ordination vows.

The School was not mentioned in the Pastoral, but the Dean and the Faculty felt it to be their duty to speak out on the subject. In January, 1924, they issued a letter to the Alumni in which they pointed out that from early times there have been divergent interpretations of some of the clauses of the Creed, as there are now, even among those who wish to enforce uniformity in the interpretation of the clause about the Virgin Birth. "There are many within the Church who could not confidently affirm a bodily ascension, or a visible coming down again of Christ from heaven for judgment, or a raising up again of their flesh, who now express through this ancient medium what they believe to be the underlying religious truths, as, for example, that Christ truly went to God to share His glory, that in Christ we face our final judge, and that God will bring us after death into eternal life. We are unable to recognize a distinction which would permit interpretation of these other clauses and deny it in the case of the Virgin Birth. The latter is simply the last of those clauses to which interpretation is applied. . . .

"We must respectfully dissent from the statement in the Pastoral that objections to the historicity of the Virgin Birth 'have been abundantly dealt with by the best scholarship of the day.' . . . The historical evidence is emphatically two-sided. . . .

"It must be recognized that many honest men and women within the Church do not find belief in the Virgin Birth essential to their whole-hearted faith in Christ and in the Incarnation. As such we hold a place within this branch of the Church of Christ. . . . To leave the Church because of dissatisfaction with clauses in the creeds would be to put the creeds above Christ and His Church, and to pursue a fruitless sectarianism."

There was a demand for 8,000 copies of this letter for wider distribution.

It was followed some months later by a small volume entitled *Creeds and Loyalty*, to which each member of the Faculty contributed a chapter. The positions taken in the letter to the Alumni were elaborated and their Biblical and historical basis presented. But by that time the Church appears to have come safely through this phase of the crisis.

The situation in which the School was left by the war was indeed discouraging. In the fall of 1920 only three new men entered. Only ten were in residence. Moreover, the School's inadequate finances were exactly where they had been a decade before. The Dean had need to face the future "indifferent to the persuasions of the discouraged." The future justified him. The next year there were nineteen students and the next thirty. In 1926 the number reached forty-one, which equalled the average enrollment of the prewar decade. In 1927 it went up to fifty-two, which was that of the record year of 1913. The average for the last ten years of Washburn's deanship was fifty-three. The peak was in 1933 when sixty-six were enrolled.

These numbers are the more significant when it is remembered that since 1933 there has been an increasingly careful scrutiny of the record of applicants for admission. A college degree has not been enough. It has had to be a degree gained with more than merely passing marks, and the holder of it must have shown qualities of character and leadership which give solid promise for the ministry.

Along with this stiffening of intellectual and moral requirements went an endeavor to deepen the spiritual life of the School. Professor Dun, addressing the Alumni in 1930, expressed the concern of his colleagues when he spoke of the need of more careful training of the student "in personal religion, the devotional life, the practice of prayer, the problems of temptation, and the sources of consolation." Said the Faculty in the *Bulletin* for April, 1931, "We are striving to give students more help in the growth of their own religious life. In the Chapel services we are constantly seeking to offer a finer experience of common prayer." Periods of directed silence in some of the Chapel services, introduced for a time by Dean Hodges and Professor Fosbroke, were revived in 1923. An annual Quiet Morning for the School, led by one of the Faculty on Matriculation Day, was begun in 1925. Another Quiet Morning at the opening of the second half-year was introduced a decade later. A second week-day Communion was added in 1932. In addition to the weekly Chapel addresses given by the Faculty in turn, Dean Washburn and Professors Drown, Addison, and Dun from time to time gave series of meditations running through several days or weekly through several weeks. A shelf of devotional books was carefully selected and the students invited to use them and guided in the more helpful ways of using them. Daily compline, led by the students, was encouraged, as were retreats for members of single classes. The first of these was arranged by the middlers in 1934. Since then most of the classes have held them annually.

In the matter of finances a striking advance was made. Indeed, the signal achievement of the early years of Washburn's deanship was the successful campaign for a million dollar endowment.

The confidence which the Dean inspired in the Alumni and in the Church at large and his tireless activity in presenting the claims of the School to the laity were major contributions to the success of the campaign, second only to the leadership of Bishop Lawrence.

We recall how Dr. Kellner had persuaded the Bishop to accept this responsibility in 1916 and how the entry of America into the war had postponed action at that time. When the campaign was resumed the Bishop again led it.

"I have been asking myself," he said, "the question which many friends and the Diocese will ask: Why do I at seventy-two years of age draw out from spiritual work in order to raise a lot of money? Why do I? The one great need of this country is leaders. While the immediate goal of this campaign is a million dollars, the real purpose is that by better equipment the School can do more effectively what her short history has proven she can do, turn out spiritual leaders."

Although the intensive campaign did not begin till January, 1923, it was preceded by almost two years of preliminary work — making the Church aware of the nature and need of theological education and of the laity's responsibility for its support. Both the Dean and the Bishop travelled over the land, preaching, addressing meetings of the Alumni, and speaking to groups of picked laymen gathered by alumni and others who were interested in the School. A committee of fifty alumni chairmen, representing different sections of the country, was organized and a publicity firm engaged. The latter had little to do except follow Bishop Lawrence's suggestions. "The Bishop," said the head of the firm, "is a genius for publicity."

Before any public appeal was made $150,000 was secured: Bishop Lawrence himself, William H. Lincoln, President of the Trustees, and Mr. Charles G. Washburn, brother of the Dean, headed the list, each with $10,000, and E. S. Rousmaniere, '86, and his wife followed with $100,000. This gift, as Mr. Lincoln said, was "a joyful surprise." It set the ball rolling.

On March 3, 1923, the campaign went "over the top." Said the Dean, "That we have done what we set out to do seems hardly real. . . . We have had revealed to us as never before the confidence not only of the Alumni but of hundreds of men and women in what the School stands for. . . . We have realized that the reason why people in general have taken little interest in theological education is because they knew nothing about it. . . . Deans of other seminaries have given us permission to come and get all we could right under their own eaves. . . . Figuratively and literally Nashotah has done almost more than it ought for Cambridge."

While most of the money subscribed was for general endowment, some was designated for specific purposes. The $100,000 given by the Rousmanieres was to endow a professorship in the New Testament; $87,000, given by the family of Robert Treat Paine, was to go toward the endowment of a chair in Christian Social Ethics, and $84,000, from churches and individuals associated with William Reed

Huntington, toward a professorship of Church History. Gifts designated for the Alumni chair of the History of Religion and Missions raised that fund to $63,000.

About $100,000 was used for the immediate erection of three new faculty houses and the purchase of the land on which they were built. They were completed in the fall of 1924 and the hitherto nameless lane on which they front was christened St. John's Road.[1] An unexpected drain on the endowment to the amount of $54,000 in 1925 was caused by the need of rebuilding the walls of Lawrence Hall, which were found to be bulging dangerously.

By the endowment the School was enabled to increase faculty salaries to meet the rapidly rising postwar cost of living, to provide for faculty pensions,[2] and to establish a system of sabbatical leaves of absence. Dean Hodges had temporarily succeeded in getting such a system started, for a few years after 1901, and again from 1910 until the first World War interrupted. Beginning with 1922 sabbaticals have been granted with almost unvarying regular-

[1] They were numbered 2, 4, and 6 and occupied respectively by Professors Dun, Muller, and Hatch. When Dun moved into the deanery in 1940, Professor Emrich came into No. 2. No. 6 is "the Rousmaniere House," named in honor of E. S. Rousmaniere, '86, whose brother-in-law gave the money for it. The land was part of what had once been Bishop Lawrence's estate. This had been sold to a gentleman who gave it to Harvard. The School purchased a part from Harvard, whose authorities at the time assured the School that while they could not bind their successors, they would go on record that it was their understanding that if the remainder of the property were ever to be sold the School should be given the first option on it.

[2] Since the establishment of the Church Pension Fund the School has paid the premiums of the Faculty. In 1934 the Trustees voted that a teacher may retire or be retired at the age of sixty-eight; he shall retire at seventy. If he is not entitled to the full benefit of the Church Pension Fund "the Trustees shall make such other provision as may appear suitable" — a phrase which is presumably to be interpreted in the light of the past practice of so supplementing the Church pensions of men ordained prior to the establishment of the Fund that their pensions shall equal those paid to men receiving the full benefit of the Fund.

ity. They have proven of great value, not only in the refreshment and stimulation brought by rest or travel, but also in the opportunity given for uninterrupted research and writing. Most of the books published by the Faculty during the past twenty years — and there have been thirty or more of them — have been written during sabbaticals.

The successful endowment campaign did not leave the School forever free from financial worries. The shrinkage of income in the depression of 1929 and the years following made it impossible for the School to maintain its Faculty at full strength or to provide as completely for scholarships and fellowships as it had hoped to do. There was an annual deficit. This was partly met by an appeal from the Dean to certain of the alumni and others for yearly gifts of $100 each, partly by income from additional legacies which the School was fortunate enough to inherit, and partly by gifts of varying amounts from the "Friends" of the School. The creation of this group was due to the suggestion in 1929 of E. A. Whitney of the Trustees. Its purpose was primarily to create intelligent interest in the School among clergy and laity, and secondarily to raise annually an unrestricted fund for the improvement of the School's work. This amounted to about $1,500 a year.

In 1931, when the balance of the Reed estate came to the School on the death of Mr. Reed's daughter-in-law, the capital funds were increased by $180,000. In 1936 they were further increased by two legacies, one of $100,000 from George S. Fiske, '98, for a chair in Theology, and one of $50,000 from Dr. Kellner for the employment of special lecturers. During the next three years two more legacies, from Marcella B. Upham and Susan Upham, amounting to $122,500, as endowment for scholarships, were received.

Much of the credit for the School's weathering the depression as well as it did is due to the wise leadership of B. Preston Clark, President of the Trustees from 1928 to 1937.

He served as a member of the Board for twenty-seven years. He was succeeded as President by Robert Amory, nephew and grandson respectively of the former Trustees, Harcourt Amory and James Sullivan Amory.

Besides the new faculty houses and the rebuilding of the walls of Lawrence Hall, the chief addition to the School's physical equipment in Dean Washburn's time was the remodelling in 1930 of the chancel of the Chapel by members of the Lawrence family in memory of the wife of the Bishop. In 1939 the Chapel was further adorned by altar hangings in memory of F. R. Kellogg, father of F. B. Kellogg, '37, and by new lights in memory of G. H. Crocker, father of Mrs. J. T. Addison. Finally, the Dean took no little satisfaction in inducing the Trustees in 1938 to invest a few thousand dollars in improving the rear of the School property, long an eyesore to the neighborhood. A lawn replaced the desert behind Reed Hall and curbing and a paved surface the quagmires of St. John's Road. The residents on that road shared the Dean's satisfaction.

Washburn's deanship was a time of changes in the pattern of Faculty-student intercourse. The Fridays at-home of Dean Hodges' days continued through the early twenties, but the increasing pressure of outside engagements made it impossible for everyone regularly to keep Friday afternoons and evenings open. Hence friendly contact between faculty families and students began to take on different forms — teas on other days and on more days, breakfasts at the deanery, crackers and cheese at bed time, strawberry festivals, and suppers in Chinatown.

Peculiarly prolific in new manifestations of social life was the decade 1930–40. School picnics began about 1930. In some years there were two, one in the spring and one in the autumn, always at least one — in the autumn on Columbus Day. Students and their "girls," Faculty and their families motored to the beach at Ipswich or to the country home of E. B. Welch, '38, near Newburyport, or to the summer place of F. C. Lawrence, '25, near Duxbury. There were outdoor games and tramps in the woods or along the beaches in the afternoon, supper around a camp fire, and songs and stunts in the evening.

In 1931 the annual spring auction of the St. John's Society began. Rummage was collected from students and Faculty and sold amid great gaiety (notably stimulated by auctioneer T. H. Chappell, '35), the proceeds going to the Missions Fund. Dean Washburn's last year's hat always brought a phenomenal price.

In 1932–33 a play, written, staged, and directed by H. I. Andrews, '36, was given by the students in several parish houses in the vicinity and $750 earned for student aid.

In 1932 A. A. Corti, '33, inaugurated the "Coffee Club": anyone, student or teacher, with a thirst for a cup of coffee between classes at eleven o'clock any day might drop into Corti's room and receive one, — a custom continued after his graduation by at least five presidents of the St. John's Society.

Then there was the annual climbing of Mt. Monadnock, sometimes in the fall, more often in the late spring after the examination period. Five or six car loads would drive to Jaffrey in the morning; after a hot-dog lunch the mountain would be climbed; then back to supper at the Hartwell Farm at Concord or a Chinese restaurant in Boston.

For all who stayed in Cambridge over the Christmas holiday there was a Swedish supper at one of the faculty houses on Christmas Eve, followed by a pilgrimage to Boston to the carol service at the Church of the Advent and then to join the outdoor carolling on Beacon Hill — every window of every house ablaze with double rows of candles.

But all this was before the days of blackouts and gasoline rationing, rubber and coffee shortage, and an accelerated schedule of studies.

XVIII

MAJORS, MINORS, PRECEPTORS, AND TUTORS

THE early years of Washburn's deanship saw striking changes in the curriculum. In the first place Greek as a requirement went by the board. This was in 1921. Most of the colleges no longer required Greek for the A.B. degree, and many men ignorant of it were coming to the School. Hence the policy was adopted of offering courses in the New Testament based on the English text, parallel to those in which the Greek text was used. However, when the School had the opportunity of advising prospective theological students who were still in college, it urged them to take Greek. If a man entirely without it had shown capacity for other languages, he was advised to study it in his first year in the School. This policy has continued to the present. About half of the men study the New Testament in Greek.

Next there was a decrease in the number of required courses and an increase in the number of electives, in order to permit some degree of specialization. To foster this a system of major and minor studies or, in the language of the committee on the curriculum, of "concentration and distribution" was introduced. While in 1920 rather less than a third of a student's work was elective, in 1921 more than half was made so. All studies were grouped in four divisions: Bible, Church History, Theology, and Practical Theology, and about two-thirds of a student's elective courses had to be concentrated in one of them, the rest distributed throughout the others. This arrangement gave elbow room to the many new subjects which had been gaining a place among elective studies during the previous decade or two: Philosophy of Religion, Normal and Abnormal Psychology, Religious Biography, Comparative Religion, Psychology of Religion, Sociology, Religious Education, Church Music. It also opened the door more widely to the wealth of courses offered in the University.

But there were drawbacks: the reduction of the time given to the required studies meant that they had to be presented in somewhat sketchy introductory courses; concentration in one division might leave a graduate almost wholly ignorant of the others. Hence after four years' trial the major and minor system was abandoned, and the number of electives reduced. Old Testament, New Testament, Church History, Theology, Preaching, and Pastoral Care remained the backbone of the course, but room was also kept for several of the newer subjects: every student was to take, some time during his three years, a course in Christian Social Ethics; a course in Religious Education; a course in Missions, and a course in either the Philosophy of Religion, or the Psychology of Religion, or the History of Religion. Additional electives represented about one-fourth of the student's work. With slight modification this has remained essentially the curriculum to the present.

In 1925 the requirement of a degree thesis was abolished except for candidates for distinction. (It was made optional even for them in 1941.)

Quite as important as changes in the curriculum have been changes in teaching method: notably a shift from the lecture to the conference and an increase in the opportunity offered to the student for individual work.

Since the School has always been small, there has always been opportunity for discussion in the classroom; and, owing to the friendly relations between students and Faculty, and the proximity of their living quarters, there has been frequent conference outside the classroom. Hence it might be argued that movements in the direction of more individualized instruction have reflected the influence of the recent practice of certain larger institutions rather than the urgent need of the School itself. However that may be, an increase in such methods has come and on the whole has proven of value.

The institutions whose practices have most directly influenced the School are Harvard and Princeton, Harvard chiefly and Princeton secondarily.

The Harvard Tutorial System involves the reduction of the number of courses taken by a student, usually from five to four, and, in place of the fifth course, a weekly meeting individually with a tutor for report and conference on whatever work the tutor has assigned, the work being such as will assist the student to coördinate his studies and deepen his knowledge of his chosen field. The Princeton Preceptorial System involves a reduction in the number of lectures in a given course, usually by a third, and the division of the class into small groups for weekly conferences with the instructor on the work of the course. This means, for the student, the replacement of one out of three hours in class by a group conference hour; for the teacher, the replacement of one lecture by two or three or more conference hours.

Dr. Muller, having been brought up on the Princeton system, used it in one or two of his courses in 1916–17, and again after his later return to the School. In 1925 he made the fatal mistake of dividing the juniors into preceptorial groups according to their scholastic standing: those in the lowest group were forthwith opprobriously dubbed by the whole School "Muller's Morons." He let subsequent classes divide themselves. Professor Washburn had also introduced a conference hour into some of his courses as early as 1916.

It was not, however, until 1938–39, when Dr. Taylor taught at Princeton for a year and returned full of enthusiasm for the Preceptorial System that it has been more widely used in the School.

The Harvard experiment, being closer at hand and readily observed, was adopted by the School for use with the senior class in 1928. Dr. Addison made a study of it and was chiefly responsible for persuading the rest of the Faculty of its virtues. He was seconded by Professor E. A. Whitney of Harvard, who had been elected a Trustee of the School in 1926, and who was one of the ablest of the Harvard tutors.

Thus it has come about that both the Preceptorial and Tutorial Systems are in use at the School, the former in some of the courses required for juniors, while seniors attend a weekly tutorial appointment in place of one course. Since 1939 a like privilege has been extended to selected middlers. There has also, in recent years, been an increased demand, especially on the part of the seniors, for reading courses, that is, courses in which the student, under the direction of one of the Faculty with whom he confers weekly, pursues a course of reading on a single topic. This has much in common with tutorial work.

It should perhaps be recalled that the "seminars" held in the eighties and nineties by Professors Steenstra and Allen, and later by Professors Nash and Drown were much like preceptorial conferences. They were not seminar courses in the present sense, but additional evening meetings of regular courses, in which papers were read and discussed. Moreover, directed individual study, in which a single student works under the guidance of a professor, was introduced in the School as early as 1891. Verily there is nothing new under the academic sun. Indeed the Preceptorial System at Princeton and the Tutorial System at Harvard are efforts to recapture for large institutions the advantages of small ones.

Along with tutoring came General Examinations and, a year later, Reading Periods. Here again the School followed Harvard. At the end of each half-year there is a period of two or three weeks when classes do not meet and the students devote themselves to additional reading in the subjects of the courses they have been taking. The General Examinations come at the end of the senior year. Three of them are written, one is oral. The written ones are in the three major fields of Bible, Church History, and Theology. The oral examination, conducted by a committee of at least three of the Faculty, is primarily for the purpose of giving a man a chance to show that he knows more than his written papers may have indicated. (Again we recall that there were general examinations in the decade 1879–89.)

In order to receive the School's degree a student, in addition to completing the work in his courses, must pass the General Examinations with an average of C+ or about seventy-eight per cent. For men whose average is below this the certificate, formerly used from 1879 to 1905, and abandoned in the latter year, was reintroduced in 1931.

Something of the new emphasis in subject matter as well as the new method may be gathered from an account of the School given to the clergy of Buffalo by Cornelius DuBois, '31, the year after he graduated. Taking for granted his hearers' understanding that the "foundation stones" of Theology, Biblical Study, and Church History, were well laid, he went on to describe what the School was doing to fit men to deal with the contemporary situation.

"Much emphasis," he said, "is laid upon preaching, upon preaching in simple, human language. . . . A course in preaching is required of every junior, middler, and senior, each year with a different instructor. Sermons must be prepared both to be passed in for criticism and to be delivered before one's classmates. . . . Each senior preaches twice at weekday service at St. Paul's Cathedral, Boston, and two or three times before the assembled School. Preaching from

Bible texts is stressed, and in the middle year each student is required to pass an examination, independently of any course, on the contents of the whole Bible.

"Pastoral Care in the first year ranges all the way from the keeping of parish records to the care of one's personal appearance. . . . For the middle year an elective course is provided giving special emphasis to the psychological and psychiatric aspects of pastoral care, and prominent doctors and psychiatrists are brought in to lecture. . . . I shall never forget the course in Pastoral Care given for the seniors by Bishop Sherrill. We met every Wednesday evening in the Dean's house, and sat around the fire in an intimate and informal way listening to the experiences and conclusions of a truly great pastor. . . .

"The Social Gospel occupies an important place in the curriculum. . . . Courses are given in such subjects as the Social Teachings of Jesus, the Church and Social Problems, and Christian Social Teaching in History, and there are seminar courses in such topics as the Family. Opportunity is given for practical social work. A large number of students last year gave up one afternoon occasionally to visit a neighboring almshouse.[1] . . . Every summer certain men attend the Cincinnati Summer School of Social Service.

"Every effort is made to keep the student abreast of the thought of the times. One of the courses that I personally got the most out of was in the psychology of religion. . . . Other courses related to the contemporary situation deal with such subjects as science and religion, the person of Christ, the value of prayer, the matter of Church unity. In the course in science and religion six or eight of us met every week at Professor Dun's house from eight to ten in

[1] Dr. Richard Cabot, at a meeting of the St. John's Society, suggested that lonely people at the "State Farm" at Tewksbury would be cheered by friendly visits from the students. Begun in 1931, such visits have continued to the present.

the evening. Ginger ale or hot chocolate was served at nine, and we talked over in a leisurely and thoughtful way the vast branches of the subject, each one doing some scientific reading in Millikan, Jeans, Pupin, and the like, and taking turns preparing papers to read.

"The feeling is growing at Cambridge that there has been too much lecturing and that what is needed is more time for individual study and research. In the senior year a chance is given to all who have attained a B average or higher to write a 10,000 word thesis on some cherished subject in place of a half course. Also in the third year each student is assigned to some member of the Faculty as his tutor, and once a week he prepares a paper and goes to the professor's house and reads it. Then tea is served and tutor and tutee talk things over. I look back on my tutorials as one of the pleasantest and most profitable parts of my whole seminary life, when I had a chance to think and discuss unhurriedly, and to refresh and stimulate and stretch my mind with the mature ideas of my tutor."

XIX

CHAIRS OLD AND NEW

WHEN Dean Washburn began his work as Dean, the Faculty, beside himself, consisted of Kellner (who was shortly to retire), Drown, Hatch, Addison, Nash, and Dun. Addison and Nash had returned from the war in 1919 and had been made Assistant Professors, the one in the History of Religion and Missions, the other in the New Testament. Angus Dun, '17, had been elected Instructor in Systematic Divinity and assistant minister of the Chapel congregation one week before Washburn was elected Dean.

From the opening of the School the chair of Homiletics and Pastoral Care, as well as the pastorship of the Chapel congregation, had been joined to the deanship, but Dean Washburn rightly felt that he ought not to be burdened with either of these duties. The deanship and the chair of Church History were more than enough. Hence there was urgent need for a professor of Pastoral Care who would also be pastor of the Chapel congregation. C. G. Twombly, '94, and W. J. Scarlett, '09, both declined the position. The next choice was Samuel McComb, canon of the Cathedral in Baltimore, an author and preacher of distinction, who had previously, for eleven years, been associated with Elwood Worcester in the Emmanuel Movement in Boston. His coming to Cambridge gave rise to the hope that the School would pioneer in the application of the New Psychology to the relief of the troubled conscience and the healing of the body and the mind. But Dr. McComb's strengths and interests proved to be elsewhere than in the classroom and after four and a half years he withdrew from the School.

This put the problem of pastoral care and preaching back into the lap of the Dean and the Faculty where it has remained ever since. What began as a temporary expedient has developed into a more or less permanent and, on the whole, successful arrangement; namely, to have some of the work in this department done by members of the Faculty of other departments, and some by men in the active ministry.

As early as 1909 Dean Hodges had invited successful parish ministers to describe their methods to the seniors. Later, when there was a suggestion of calling a full-time assistant to the Dean in this field, he advised, rather, the employment of active clergy as part-time lecturers. Much of the instruction in medical schools is given by practising physicians, why not utilize practising ministers in the theological school?

It is this policy which the School has employed for the last seventeen years. Some of the instruction has been given at different times by Dean Washburn and Professors Addison and Dun, and recently by Professor Emrich, but much of it has been given by practising clergy. Among them, to name only those who have taught for three or more years, have been Bishops Lawrence and Sherrill, Archdeacon Dennen, Dean Sturges of St. Paul's Cathedral, P. E. Osgood of Emmanuel Church, Boston, A. C. Lichtenberger of St. Paul's, Brookline, Raymond Calkins of the First Congregational Church, Cambridge, C. L. Glenn of Christ Church, Cambridge, D. R. Hunter, Chaplain of the Massachusetts General Hospital, and Otis R. Rice (now Chaplain of St. Luke's Hospital, New York). The longest in service was Dean Sturges, whose thirteen years of teaching were ended by his death in 1940. Moreover, many of the students have profited by the Harvard courses in the Study of Personality given by the late Dr. Richard Cabot and in Preaching by Dean Sperry and Dr. Park.

An experiment was made during the years 1928–32 with

an elective course in Pastoral Care in which five or six specialists in different fields — physicians, as well as clergymen — each gave four or five lectures. Subjects such as ministry to the sick, the problems of youth, work with juvenile delinquents, with prisoners, with the mentally troubled were discussed. It was found, however, that the course lacked coherence and that the subjects presented could be more effectively dealt with, some in the normal courses on Pastoral Care, some in courses in Psychology, and some in the courses given by the Chaplain of the Massachusetts General Hospital, which involved actual ministration to the sick, under his direction. This clinical training at the hospital was begun in 1933.

Other departments beside that of Practical Theology were strengthened in Dean Washburn's time.

In 1921 Mrs. May Sleeper Ruggles, "Ma Ruggles" as she was affectionately called, began instruction in the use of the voice. Although a part-time teacher, she gave so much of her time to the School and took such a lively interest in the students that they came to look upon her as an indispensable part of the School's life. There was hardly a man whose reading and speaking she did not improve. With some she worked marvels. The genuineness of her concern for them led many to seek her advice on problems quite unconnected with the voice. For nineteen years, till her retirement in 1938, she exercised a real ministry in the School.

A full-time instructor in Church Music was employed for the first and as yet only time in the School's history from 1922 to 1925. A. Vincent Bennett, who filled this post, was an enthusiast for religious drama as well as music; and pageants and miracle plays illumine his brief term of service in the memory of the men who were here at the time. In 1925 he was ordained and went into the parish ministry, and the Trustees, having received no endowment for full-time musical instruction, felt they were not warranted in continuing it. Part-time instruction under R. G. Appel, the former organist and part-time instructor, was resumed.

After Dr. Kellner's retirement in 1922 the School depended, for instruction in the Old Testament, on special lecturers and on Harvard courses until Charles Lincoln Taylor, Jr., '24, was ready to take over the work. A graduate of Williams and Oxford, assistant at St. John's, Waterbury, for a year after graduation from the School, he became a teaching fellow and assistant pastor of the Chapel congregation in 1925, instuctor in 1930, Assistant Professor in 1932, the year he earned his Th.D. at Harvard, and Professor in 1937.

In order to relieve the Dean of some of his ever increasing burden, J. A. Muller, '10, was called as Professor of Church History and Lecturer in Liturgics and Polity in 1923. A graduate of Princeton and the School, he had held the A. V. G. Allen fellowship for study in Europe; had been an instructor at the School, 1914–17, and had subsequently taught at Boone University in China, at St. Stephens College, and at the General Theological Seminary.

One of the announced objects of the endowment campaign was the establishment of a chair in Christian Sociology. As Dr. Drown said at the time, "It is of vital importance that the School take a position of strong Christian leadership in the social and economic problems of the time. If it fails to lead in this respect it will lose its opportunity to serve the Church in the coming generation. Nothing could be more disastrous than such a failure."

Neither the subject nor the realization of the duty to teach it was new in the School. Said Dean Hodges, in 1905: "Beside the chair of Theology must stand the chair of Sociology in order that men may read intelligently in the open book of modern life. . . . Twenty years ago the center of modern interest was in the relation between religion and science; ten years ago it was in the relation between religion and Scripture; at this moment the heart of the situation is in the relation between religion and society." R. A. Woods, as we recall, had lectured in Sociology from 1895 to 1914. From 1917 to 1922 P. G. Kammerer, '12, assistant at Emmanuel Church, Boston, did the same. Moreover, the courses at Harvard under Dr. Richard Cabot, Professor of Social Ethics, 1920–34, and his assistant, from 1920 to 1924, the Rev. Niles Carpenter, who had studied at the School with the class of '20, were courses in which Christian ethics were given a prominent place. They were elected by many of the School's students.

Meanwhile Norman Burdett Nash, '15 (Harvard '09), who had followed his father in the teaching of the New Testament, was also following him in his interest in the social message of the New Testament, and in 1923 the words "Instructor in Christian Social Ethics" were placed after his New Testament title. The next year he studied abroad, and in 1925 his titles were reversed and he became Assistant Professor (in 1927 Professor) of Christian Social Ethics and Lecturer in the New Testament. This combination of sound New Testament scholarship with a growing knowledge of Sociology proved a peculiarly happy one, and Nash's courses were among the most stimulating in the School, as was his playing of touch-football with the students the most vigorous and volcanic. To the universal regret of Trustees, Faculty, Alumni, and students he resigned in 1939 to become Rector of St. Paul's School, Concord, New Hampshire.

The department of Theology was strengthened by the addition of William Lawrence Wood, '13. He was born in New York in 1887. He graduated from Columbia in 1908. Like Dean Gray he always remained something of a New Yorker; he used to say that the best thing in Boston was the five o'clock train for New York. He studied abroad for two

years on a fellowship from the School, was successively
rector at Lenox, Massachusetts, Red Cross Chaplain in
France, rector at Santa Paula, California, and at Waban,
Massachusetts. In 1924–25, while at Waban, he was a lecturer at the School. In 1926 he became rector at Ross,
California, and professor at the Church Divinity School of
the Pacific. In 1929 he was made a lecturer at the School
and in 1933, Professor of the Philosophy of Religion. On
his birthday, January 10, 1936, while crossing Brattle Street
to attend morning chapel, he was struck by an automobile.
Six days later he died from concussion of the brain.

Fifteen years before, Bishop McCormick, when recom-
mending Wood for a rectorship, characterized him as "one
of the most promising young men I know, a good preacher,
scholarly, and a gentleman in the best sense of the word.
His only limitation is absentmindedness."

This was a limitation he never outgrew. Although he
was but forty-nine at his death, a tall, vigorous, athletic man
who liked to play tennis and football with the students, he
was, at the same time, the perfect exemplar of the absent-
minded professor.

His borrowing of books from the library in such quan-
tities that they had to be returned by the car load at the end
of the term, and his pencilling marginal comments in them
were the despair of the librarian; his unsystematic, rumina-
tive, explosive manner in the classroom was the despair of
the less philosophically-minded students; his casual, irre-
sponsible forgetfulness of appointments was the despair of
the Dean. But he was a grand person, warm-hearted,
friendly, original in his thinking, provocative in his suggestions, and endlessly diverting in his absent-mindedness.

Some of his doings were epic. There was the time he
drove into Boston with two of his children, left them in
his car on Beacon Street, locked in for safety, while he
went shopping, and came back to Cambridge on the sub-

way. Then there was the day he stepped into his car at Harvard Square, drove home and, on opening his garage, found his car already there. He notified the police that he had taken somebody's car by mistake and they came for it. That evening when he was about to leave the house and put on his hat he discovered that it was not his hat at all — it was one he had picked up in the car he had driven home that afternoon.

Those who knew him best bear testimony to a new integration of purpose and a fresh release of power which came to him from his experience in his last years with the Oxford Groups. "He was," says one who met him the summer before his death, "the happiest man I have ever seen — so full of faith in God and in himself, so confident and so radiant. . . . Oddly enough, his death is the first I have ever met with which has left me with a feeling of the essential unimportance of death. . . . He does not seem dead at all but only part of something which is deathless and eternal."

Dr. Drown's retirement in 1933, followed by Wood's death in 1936, put the entire burden of the Department of Theology upon Dun. In 1937 Richard S. M. Emrich was elected an instructor in this field. On graduation from Brown, he had spent a year in the School in the class of '35, but finished at Union. He then took a Ph.D. at Marburg. His interests and studies led him increasingly into the field of Social Ethics and in 1940 he was elected Assistant Professor in that subject, as a successor to Norman Nash, at the same time continuing some teaching in Theology.

The last year of Washburn's deanship was marked by further faculty changes: J. T. Addison resigned to become First Vice-President of the National Council, in charge of Foreign Missions, and two new members of the Faculty were elected.

James Thayer Addison, a classmate of Norman Nash at

Harvard, taught for a year after his graduation in St. John's University, Shanghai. After graduation from the School in 1913, he served two years in domestic mission work in Oklahoma. He became an instructor at the School in 1915, Assistant Professor in 1919, and Professor in 1926. In addition to teaching the History of Religion and Missions, he instructed the juniors in preaching with signal success for a dozen years; he shouldered more than his share of tutoring; and, as has been noted, was largely responsible for the introduction of the Tutorial System into the School.

He was enabled to perfect his knowledge of his chosen subjects in the free time arranged for him by the Trustees: following a plan in operation at Yale, they allowed him a half-year's leave of absence after each two and a half years' teaching. Thus he had opportunity to live and study in China, Japan, Egypt, and Syria. He has produced several notable books in his field.

His training and experience have fitted him superbly for the oversight of the foreign missions of the Church. But the Church's gain has been the School's sore loss.

The two new members of the Faculty, elected in 1940, were Sherman E. Johnson and Massey H. Shepherd, Jr. Dr. Johnson, a graduate of Northwestern University and the Seabury-Western Theological Seminary, received his Ph.D. from the University of Chicago in 1936, and taught at Nashotah House for four years before coming to the School as Assistant Professor of the New Testament. Dr. Shepherd is a graduate of the University of South Carolina and a Ph.D. from the University of Chicago in 1937. He taught three years in the University of Chicago Divinity School before coming to Cambridge as Instructor in Church History. In 1942 he became Assistant Professor.

Since the work of a theological school is primarily that of training future clergy, its contribution to the education of contemporary clergy and of the laity is often overlooked.

The School has long been active in these spheres. Ever since there have been summer conferences on religion, whether for clergy or laity, members of the Faculty and Alumni have lectured at them. What is now the Wellesley Conference began at the School and only moved to Wellesley when attendance became so numerous that quarters at the School were no longer adequate. Summer Conferences at Albany, at Concord, at Blue Mountain, at Geneva, at Sweet Briar, and occasionally at places still farther afield, have numbered professors from the School among their teachers, and there is probably no conference in the country at which alumni have not taught.

Moreover, during the school year, the Faculty has frequently been engaged in extension teaching. Dean Hodges gave courses all over the country. In 1906 and 1907 the Massachusetts Sunday School Commission arranged for courses for the laity to be given by the Faculty in Boston. In 1908 and subsequent years Monday afternoon lectures for neighboring clergy were given at the School. Early in Washburn's deanship seminars for clergy, meeting one afternoon a week, were provided, and more recently the "Kellner Lectures" have been scheduled at times when clergy could attend. In 1932 began the annual "Cambridge Lectures," sponsored by the Massachusetts Department of Religious Education: they are courses for the laity given each fall by three members of the Faculty in three different centers in the diocese.

The Faculty have, also, from time to time, taught at the College of Preachers in Washington, and on four occasions between 1925 and 1932 one was sent by the Trustees to California at the invitation of the Church Divinity School to give an intensive course (lecturing twice daily) between Christmas and the opening of the second half-year. Dr. Drown taught at Boone and St. John's Universities in China during a sabbatical; Dr. Addison did the same there as well as at the American University in Cairo, and the American University at Beirut. Recently Dr. Taylor taught at Princeton University, commuting thither weekly; Dr. N. B. Nash did the same at Yale, and Dr. Shepherd at the Berkeley Divinity School.

From the opening of the School practically every Sunday has found every member of the Faculty conducting service and preaching somewhere. As has already been noted, the Dean was pastor of the Chapel congregation except for the four years of Dr. McComb's tenure. After McComb's resignation it was increasingly felt that the merger of this congregation with that of Christ Church was greatly to be desired; a single strong parish, instead of two which were not so strong within a few blocks of each other, would more than double the impact of the Church on both the community and the University. On January 1, 1930, the merger was consummated and the results have surpassed the anticipations of those who effected it.

Another merger which Dean Washburn had hoped to accomplish was that of the Cambridge and the Berkeley Schools. This had been suggested as early as 1902 by Dean Hodges, himself a graduate of Berkeley, but at that time Berkeley showed no interest. In 1928, when Berkeley was contemplating removal from Middletown, Dean Washburn renewed the suggestion with similar results. But in 1934 Dean Ladd of Berkeley suggested to Dean Washburn that perhaps the time had come to resume the discussion. This led first to informal conferences, then in 1935 to the formal appointment of conference committees representing the Trustees, Faculty, and Alumni of both Schools, and to the passage of an act in the Connecticut legislature, at the request of Berkeley, permitting Berkeley to move to Cambridge if and when it desired to do so.

It appears that the Berkeley Trustees were never unanimously in favor of the merger, although a majority voted to empower their committee to negotiate "to the end that these two New England Schools may be combined under one management in Cambridge, with a suitable name which shall preserve our identity. . . . A representation of the Trustees from this board shall be chosen for the board of the combined schools; positions on the Faculty shall be given to Dean Ladd, Dr. Hedrick, and Dr. James, with salaries and residences equal to those now granted in the Cambridge School."

It was understood that the Berkeley funds were sufficient to finance the "salaries and residences" of the three Berkeley professors, but on further examination it became evident that they were not. Other matters, such as a new name and a revised organization, were worked out to the apparent satisfaction of all concerned, but since the Cambridge School was, at the time, operating under an annual deficit, it was not in a position to accept further financial responsibility. Hence the Berkeley conference committee proposed to the Berkeley Trustees that only two Berkeley professors (Dean Ladd and one other) be contributed to the combined School. A majority of the Berkeley Trustees voted No to the merger on this basis and terminated negotiations in October, 1935. A factor contributing to their decision appears to have been an increased willingness to support Berkeley in New Haven on the part of several of its alumni and friends — a willingness awakened by the news of its possible removal to Cambridge.

"I am deeply disappointed with the decision," wrote Dean Washburn to Dean Ladd. "For many years I have dreamed of a strong joint school conserving the traditions of both yours and ours. Now I must abandon the vision." To Preston Clark he wrote: "I feel now as I have for the last fifteen years, that it is a great pity that two schools so much alike and so near together should not combine, so that the drain on the Church might be less, and the overhead in the education of each man be greatly reduced." [1]

Deep as Dean Washburn's disappointment may have been at the failure of the merger with Berkeley, it must have been a supreme satisfaction to him on his retirement at Commencement, 1940, when 200 Alumni turned out to express their admiration and affection, that the School of which he had been given the leadership in the difficult days of 1920, was now in a thriving condition.

The enrollment during his last year was sixty-two. The opening of that year saw the largest number of entering juniors — twenty-seven — as well as the largest number of men entering all classes — thirty-six — in the history of the School.

Although two of the ablest members of the Faculty had left, two young men of promise had been elected; the Trustees were capably led by Robert Amory, and the future deanship of the School was in the hands of Angus Dun.

[1] Some alumni on the Pacific coast suggested at the time that Berkeley come to Berkeley, California, and combine with the Church Divinity School there, which was in need of whatever assistance Berkeley might bring and could appropriately change its name to "The Berkeley Divinity School."

XX

KELLNER AND DROWN

D<small>R.</small> K<small>ELLNER</small> died on August 6, 1935; Dr. Drown on
January 24, 1936. Each was seventy-four years old.

Maximilian Lindsay Kellner or, as he preferred to be
called, Max Kellner, was born in Detroit in 1861. He graduated from Hobart College, where his father was a professor, in 1881. Then, at the urging of William Stevens Perry,
Bishop of Iowa, who had been a professor and President of
Hobart before election to the episcopate, he entered the
theological department of Griswold College, Iowa. On
graduation in 1884 he came to Cambridge to study Hebrew,
Aramaic, Assyrian, and Arabic. He enrolled as a partial
student in the School and as a senior in the University,
whence he received an A.B. in 1885 and an A.M. in 1886.
That year the School gave him a B.D. *honoris causa*, as of
the class of 1885, and made him an instructor in Hebrew.
He became Assistant Professor in 1889 and Professor ten
years later.

Until he married in 1905, he lived in No. 17 Lawrence
Hall. No. 18 housed his library. Thus living and eating
with the students for twenty years, he became the intimate
friend of a larger number than probably any other member
of the Faculty in the history of the School.

He served twice as acting-Dean; he was Secretary of the
Faculty for twenty-three years, necrologist of the Alumni
for twenty-seven, teacher in the School for thirty-six.

There is universal testimony to his extraordinary skill as
an instructor in Hebrew. He actually made men like it. For

several years that was his main work. With the decreasing demand for Hebrew after it became an elective study and with Dr. Steenstra's retirement, a considerable portion of Kellner's teaching was in the field of Biblical literature and interpretation. Those of us who sat under him in these courses did not, I fear, take them very seriously, although, thanks to the fullness and clarity of the printed outlines he gave us, we learned a good deal. His lectures were the product of the most accurate and painstaking scholarship, but we were amused by his habit of dictating them word for word, his pausing to see that we missed no syllable, and his indicating with meticulous care even the punctuation we were to use. "Period," he would say, "parenthesis," "semicolon," "comma," "dash." This was celebrated in the faculty song:

> Here's to our beloved Kelly
> Who wears a watch chain across his — breast.
> The poor Old Testament he smashes
> And leaves us nothing but commas and dashes!

In 1894 Dr. Steenstra gave this discerning estimate of Kellner: "He lacks the philosophical grasp of theology which is needed to mediate between the results of modern Biblical science and Christian doctrine at the present time, and the lack is not one of attainments merely, but of natural aptitude. For the teaching of the Hebrew, however, and for helpful instruction in the reading and understanding of the Old Testament writings, it would be difficult to find a better man." His published works were exhaustive outline studies intended chiefly for distribution to his students.

It was outside of class that those who did not study Hebrew came to appreciate him — his kindliness, his consideration, his unfailing courtesy, his thoughtfulness, his charming hospitality, his friendly, helpful manner. He was a perfect host, and his friends, as Dean Washburn said, always looked forward to him as a guest whom they thought themselves fortunate to entertain.

His interest in and loyalty to the School were proverbial. As a result of his suggestion and persuasion the School was given the library building by Mr. Wright. To him were due the fine chancel windows in the Chapel, placed there in 1917, in memory of his parents and his wife. He never hesitated to ask people to remember the School in their wills and he was irritated with them when they were not inclined to do so. In his own will he left the School $50,000, the interest of which was to be used to engage special lecturers. In this he had the double purpose of bringing to the School from time to time men of distinction who were serving in other institutions, and of making it possible for the School to give the Faculty regular sabbaticals without fear of leaving unfilled gaps in the curriculum.

One of the classic events in the history of the School was the farewell party at Professor Washburn's house in 1913, when Kellner went off for a year to Egypt and Palestine. A "Kellner Archaeological Expedition" was staged in anticipation by the students. The Washburn children's sand box was the desert; D. R. Magruder, '14, impersonated Dr. Kellner; H. K. Sherrill, '14, Mrs. Kellner; I. H. Hughes, '14, Kellner's son, Waldo, and W. L. Wood, '13, the camel. Excavation for antiquities in the desert sands produced a copy of Kellner's outline studies of Isaiah.

Kellner retired, because of a weak heart, in 1922, but for thirteen years thereafter he remained a member of the School family, regularly attending chapel, entertaining the students, taking part in all the common activities of the School, and never losing his enthusiasm for it. He worked steadily at a volume on magic and its relation to religion, which he completed, but for which he was unable to find a publisher.

Dr. Drown holds the record for the longest teaching life in the history of the School, and he was proud of it. Steenstra served actively for thirty-nine years, Allen for forty, Drown for forty-four. He retired in 1933, but in 1935 offered to give a seminar on the Atonement. His offer was gladly accepted. Eight students took it and, to Drown's delight, for the first time in all his teaching, there was a perfect attendance at every meeting. The last session of the seminar was a month before his death, and the eight members of it carried his body to the grave. As student, instructor, professor, and professor emeritus, his life had centered at the School for almost half a century.

Edward Staples Drown was born in 1861 in New Haven, where his father was rector of St. Paul's Church. His boyhood was spent in Philadelphia, Lynn, and Newburyport, whither his father moved. He graduated from Harvard with highest honors in philosophy in 1884. While there he had come under the influence of Phillips Brooks and decided to study for the ministry. In order to earn money to do so he taught for a year at Holderness School in New Hampshire, and then, because his father was temporarily blinded by cataracts, served for two years as his lay-reader while he was rector at St. Augustine, Florida. Here Drown began reading in theology and entered the middle class at the School in 1887, graduating two years later. He was chosen as an instructor immediately on graduation.

Said Bishop Lawrence, "When we first thought about him [as a possible teacher] I went to see Professor Palmer [of Harvard]. He said, 'I have had no man his superior and I do not know that I can say that I have ever had a man his equal in my department of philosophy.'" The committee of the Trustees, who were appointed in 1892 to consider whether it would be Drown or someone else who should take full responsibility for the teaching of theology, reported that "he exhibited such aptness for theology while a student in the School that he was the first choice of Dean Gray and other members of the Faculty to be instructor. Then in these three years he has shown himself strong and clear as a teacher; he has won and held the respect of his pupils who were, only the year before, his fellow students." He was, thereupon, made Assistant Professor and all the teaching of theology put in his hands. In 1899 he was made Professor. He continued to win and hold the respect of his pupils to the last, nor did he ever cease to be "strong and clear as a teacher."

He published four small books, the most considerable of which and the one which best illustrates his thought is *The Creative Christ*. His students regret that he did not publish more. But he had scant time for writing. Thrown into teaching immediately on the completion of his undergraduate course in theology, he had to do his "graduate study" while he taught, and he taught all the doctrine, ethics, and apologetics at the School, without assistance, for twenty-eight years, from 1892 to 1920. In addition to this he was the assistant minister of the Chapel congregation for twenty years, from 1889 to 1909, and from 1895 to 1902 he conducted a course in the Bible at Wellesley, going there twice a week.

He taught for thirty-four years before he had a sabbatical. When he took one, in 1923–24, he spent a good part of it teaching at Boone and St. John's Universities in China. This use of it is perhaps an indication that he felt that his gift was that of teaching, not writing, and that he would not have written more, even if he had had time for it. However that may be, there can be no question that he was a great teacher. It is hard to imagine anyone surpassing the clarity, the simplicity, the balance, the frankness, the honesty, the profound religious conviction with which he taught. It was a just tribute to him that S. M. Dorrance, '08, gave at the Alumni Dinner in 1933. "He never," said Dorrance, "pretended not to catch what you said, and answer some other question than that which you had put."

When T. R. Ludlow, '11, came to his decision to study for the ministry, J. H. Melish, '98, said to him, "Go to Cambridge and do as I did: light your candle at the flame of Dr. Nash, and Dr. Drown will show you how to carry it so that others will be guided by its light." There were many, however, who not only learned from Drown how to carry their candle; they lit it at his flame. It may not have flared as brilliantly as did Henry Sylvester Nash's at times, but it burned steadily and it burned bright.

Norman Nash described the quality of Drown's teaching thus: "Always based on careful, scholarly study, always thoroughly prepared, well planned, with the time properly proportioned, ever lucid, ever persuasive and never coercive, it was in all these ways a model. It was also, as is not always true of teaching in theology, constantly religious in spirit and in purpose. In the classroom he taught and never preached; yet his teaching had the realism of religious conviction. His favorite saying, that no doctrine is a Christian doctrine which does not spring from the experience of God in Christ and does not apply to the Christian life, was exemplified in his own teaching of theology. . . .

"He was no phrase-maker, so we have often preached and taught what we learned from him, hardly aware how much we owed him. One of our number recently told me of his own surprise when after some years he looked through his theology notes and discovered there almost everything he had been preaching."

When Drown had completed his few months' teaching at Boone University in 1923, Bishop Roots wrote: "Drown's visit to Boone was perfectly splendid. . . . This kind of thinking and teaching is about as fundamental as any work that can be done in China. . . . And better than what he said, his hearers caught something of his wonderful spirit of humility and faith and love."

His hearers in Cambridge as well as those in Wuchang caught this. As Norman Nash put it, "His life was of one piece, an integrity; and it was a very holy life." But Drown himself would have been the last person in the world to suppose that there was anything holy about it. He was an unsuspecting saint, a genial companion, a hospitable host, informal, easily approached, with a rare sense of quiet humor. It was he who treasured all the absurd and delightful stories about the earlier teachers at the School — Stone and Wharton and Gray and Steenstra and Allen — and he invariably illumined his lectures in theology by allusions to *Alice in Wonderland*.

His birthday was St. Thomas' Day, December 21, and in 1932, when he was seventy years old, the students saw to it that the Christmas play was given on that day. It was wholly devoted to him. George Shriver, '32 (now missionary at Dornakal, India), his hair whitened with talcum powder and a bristly gray mustache attached to his upper lip, impersonated the Doctor. After some practice he was able to reproduce his slightly lisping speech in which r's for the most part were elided or became w's. ("Pa'don me, Henwy, if I speak fwankly" was his invariable preface when, at Faculty meetings, he was about to disagree with Dean Washburn.) Shriver, as the Doctor, gave a lecture in Theology in which the inevitable references to *Alice in Wonderland* as well as other classic illustrations such as the "Bwutal Bwockton Murder" were simultaneously acted out in shadow pictures behind a sheet.

The great scene (written by J. T. Addison) was the Faculty meeting. In the words of the stage direction, "The Faculty is seated around a table, the Dean at one end, Drown in the center, facing the audience." And, believe it or not, the Faculty were seated around the table, for Meredith B. Wood, '32 (now Rector of Hoosac School) had persuaded them to impersonate themselves — all but Dr. Drown. The subject for discussion was the Bulletin Board. Unbecoming notices, it was said, had been appearing on it; hence the suggestion that a glass door and a lock be added to it. When Drown finally got a chance to break into the discussion it was on this wise:

"What seems to me the vital point is this. It's not a question of a good bulletin boa'd or a bad bulletin boa'd. (Pa'don me, Henwy, if I speak fwankly.) It's a matter of pwinciple. A supweme pwinciple is involved here. It is very clea'ly the pwinciple of Justification by Faith — the pwinciple of Chwistian fweedom. The old bulletin boa'd may be ugly but it's fwee to all, fwee to saints and sinners alike. It makes no false distinctions between sacwed and secular. But suppose you put up a glass case and a lock, immediately you intwoduce wules and wegulations — the whole appawatus of ecclesiastical legalism. And we might as well face it — that means casuistwy — mowal casuistwy, wight here in our cloister, and I for one pwotest."

"Well," said another member of the Faculty, "we could have a second bulletin board for student notices."

"That's just it," retorted Drown. "Of course you can. But there you violate another pwofound pwinciple. You intwoduce a double standa'd of mowality. What is wight for one bulletin boa'd is wwong for the other. Pa'don me, Henwy, if I speak fwankly, but I can see nothing but loss in giving up all our pwinciples and thwowing overboa'd the doctwine of Justification by Faith."

Like all Faculty meetings, it ended by the Dean suggesting that we have a cup of tea.

Dr. and Mrs. Drown sat in the front row and enjoyed it all hugely. At the end of the evening they were presented with a silver vase from Faculty and students, which but feebly expressed the School's affection for them both.

Mrs. Drown, now living just across the street from the School on Phillips Place, continues to keep open house daily for all its members. That she has remained, as indeed she always has been, an institution in herself, was witnessed by the depiction of one of her tea parties at the Christmas play in 1940. The student who impersonated her sang these verses, written by C. H. Buck, Jr., '41:

MRS. DROWN'S SONG
To the tune of Little Buttercup in PINAFORE

I'm extra-curricular,
Extra particular,
Cultured and charming and gay;
My knowledge spectacular,
Almost oracular,
Colors each word that I say.

I can quote you from Dante
And Emily Brontë,
I know Robert Browning by heart.
Every Portuguese sonnet
Is under my bonnet;
I'm a demon on classical art.

From the Biblical Psalms
To the music of Brahms
I can hum every theme and each air.
I've memorized Gibbon,
And here's the blue ribbon
My brownies received at the Fair.

And so to my parlor
Each teacher and scholar
Repairs for his five o'clock tea.
But I have a suspicion
They come for nutrition,
And only half listen to me.

XXI

DEAN DUN

DEAN STONE, Dean Gray, Dean Lawrence all had a good deal to say in the nomination of their successors. Dean Washburn declined to do so. Having come to an end, he decided that it should be an end, and that he ought not to have a determining hand or even a finger in the new beginning.

The Trustees canvassed all possibilities with diligence, and on March 28, 1940, elected Angus Dun. The first person whom the writer recalls nominating Dun was Max Kellner, who did so over a decade before his election. How much effect this friendly conversational propaganda had, we are unable to say. Perhaps Dean Dun is another of the many good things for which we have to thank Max Kellner.

On Commencement Day, 1940, the day Washburn retired, Dun was inaugurated. Born in New York City in 1892, he graduated from Yale in 1914. He came directly to the School and during his course acted as assistant to Professor Hocking of the Department of Philosophy at Harvard. On graduation in 1917 he became vicar of St. Andrew's, Ayer, Massachusetts, and civilian chaplain at Camp Devens. At the end of the war he was made associate secretary of the inter-church Committee on the War and the Religious Outlook. He studied at Oxford and Edinburgh in 1919–20 and at Marburg in 1926–27. Beginning his teaching at the School in 1920, as assistant to Dr. Drown in the department of Theology, he became Assistant Professor in 1922 and Professor in 1928. He assisted in the pastorate of the Chapel congregation in 1920–22 and again in 1929–30.

He was a delegate of the Episcopal Church to the Edinburgh Conference on Faith and Order, serving as secretary of the American Theological Commission in preparation for the Conference, and is a member of the Commission on Unity of the Federal Council, and of the Commissions on Faith and Order and on Approaches to Unity of the Episcopal Church. He is the author of six books.

The beginning of his deanship was marked by a salutary change in the daily schedule of School life. Hitherto chapel had begun at 8.30 A.M., following breakfast, except when the Holy Communion was administered; then the order was reversed, the service coming at eight. By the new arrangement chapel comes every morning at eight; breakfast follows. This regularity in time encourages regularity in attendance. A welcome break in routine has been introduced by omitting morning chapel on Saturday. The evening service continues to be held, as it has been for some years, daily except Saturday at 5.45.

In dealing with the perennial problem of finances Dean Dun's Scottish inheritance seems to have come to his aid. He has economized in operating expenses by inaugurating cafeteria service in the refectory. He has persuaded persons interested in Religious Education to pledge the salary of a professor in that subject for at least three years. He has combined various groups of annual givers with the "Friends" of the School and so put before them the School's needs that where formerly they were all together contributing about $3,500 annually, they now contribute about $6,000.

In 1941 the class of 1916 began what is devoutly hoped will become a precedent, namely the presentation of a substantial twenty-fifth reunion gift to the School. The classes of 1940 and 1941 initiated the practice of taking out insurance policies for the future benefit of the School. To the agreeable surprise of everyone, including the Dean, the School received a wholly unsuspected legacy of $170,000 in 1942.[1]

Apart from the problem of finances, which the present unprecedented low rate of interest on invested funds makes peculiarly pressing, other problems confronting the new dean have been the admission of women to the School, the teaching of Religious Education, and the war.

What to many may seem like a revolutionary step for an Episcopal seminary was the admission of qualified women to courses in the School in the fall of 1940.

The first feminine knock upon the School's gates was in 1921. Then a young woman, a college graduate who had completed two years' study in theology and who was fitting herself to become a teacher of the Bible, applied for admission as a special student. Her application was not favorably received. In 1935 two women, both college graduates, one of them a Master of Arts, made a similar application. It was then agreed that if they registered at Radcliffe College they might attend courses at the School. This they did, their status in the School being essentially the same as that of Harvard students taking one or more of the School's courses.

From 1935 to 1940 there were one or two — usually two — Radcliffe students studying in the School under these conditions. For the most part, however, they were but nominally Radcliffe students: although registered there, all their studies were theological. Hence it seemed to be a more straightforward procedure to admit such students directly to the School. Moreover, with the increasing employment of women as directors of religious education in our churches, and as teachers of religion in schools and colleges, the larger question arose as to whether it were not the School's duty

[1] The present endowment of the School is approximately two and a half millions which includes the plant, which is valued at about $640,000.

to the Church to offer such women training of as high a quality as that offered to men. Women are, however, as yet admitted only as special students, not candidates for the degree. Nor are they in residence.

The problem of "Religious Education" is one of long standing. Alumni were urging the creation of a chair in "Religious Pedagogy," as they called it, when the campaign for endowment was contemplated in 1917. When the campaign finally got under way in 1922–23, the Trustees, in their publicity, said that $100,000 of the endowment would be set aside for such a chair. The difficulty was to find a man to fill it. Many and various have been the experiments with part-time lecturers, as well as with courses in the Harvard School of Education. The latter, despite their general excellence, were only secondarily or remotely connected with religion. Meanwhile, the exigencies of the depression as well as the passing of the years made the Trustees forgetful of their good intention to earmark $100,000 for a chair in Religious Education. Hence, when Dean Dun tackled the problem he had to find both the man and the money.

Recognizing in Professor Adelaide T. Case of Columbia University the foremost authority on Religious Education in the Church if not in the country, he engaged her as Kellner Lecturer in the year 1940–41. Her work in this position convinced him that she was the "man" for the place. He then succeeded in securing guarantees for her salary for at least three years from persons interested in this phase of theological training. She was elected "Professor of Christian Education" in 1941.

The election of a woman to a theological faculty in the Episcopal Church seems quite as revolutionary a step as the admission of women to theological courses. But here again, it is not so revolutionary as it seems. As early as 1899–1901 Miss Sarah H. Hooker gave instruction in the use of the voice. From 1921 to 1938 Mrs. Ruggles did the same. From

1934 to 1937 Miss Mildred Hewitt and Miss Erna B. Blaydow, directors of neighboring Church Schools, were employed as part-time instructors in Religious Education. Although none of these women held the rank of professor, they were all teachers of theological students.

The seventy-fifth anniversary of the School, like the fiftieth, found the country at war. One effect of this was a summer session. In line with accelerated programs in colleges and graduate schools, the School for the first time in its history held such a session in 1942. It counted as an academic half-year. Beginning on June 15, it continued for twelve weeks. Daily morning chapel was at seven, instead of eight, breakfast at seven-thirty, with classes on five days a week, beginning at eight. The junior class entered in June. The seniors graduated in February, 1943. A second summer session was held in 1943.

The early effect of the war on the enrollment was markedly different from that of 1917, although the ultimate effect may yet be the same. In 1917–18 the tendency was for most of the students, other than seniors, and practically all prospective students, to join the armed forces. The result, as we have seen, was a student body of eight within a little over a year after America's entry into the war. At the beginning of the present war the government, the colleges, and the Churches, urged men to continue with their education unless or until they were called out, and theological students were exempted from the draft. Hence the decrease in enrollment was not nearly so precipitous as in 1918. In the fall of 1941 the enrollment was seventy, the largest in the history of the School. In the summer session of 1942, it was sixty-one. In the fall of 1942, it was fifty-seven. And this drop was not due primarily to the war, for but seven students left to join the armed forces between 1941 and 1943. It was due chiefly to the Faculty's increasingly intensive scrutiny of both the men who were in the School and those applying for entrance. They felt that the exemption of the theological student from military service should mean that no man be admitted who does not show unmistakable promise for the ministry and no man retained who does not live willingly under as exacting a discipline as his fellows in the army. The lowering of the draft age to eighteen in 1942, not to mention other influences, is now in the process of reducing if not drying up entirely the stream of entering men. In February, 1943, the School was reduced to forty-two; in October, 1943, to thirty-seven. If the war continues it may once again shrivel to its 1918 proportions.

"The test of an educational institution," said Bishop Lawrence at the time of the endowment campaign, "is not in the teachers, but in what the teachers manufacture; the test is in the graduates." And he pointed with confidence to the School's record in training for leadership. Of the 450 living graduates at that time the great majority, he said, were hard at work in city and village as pastors and community leaders. Among them were also six deans of cathedrals, seven headmasters of schools, one college president, and fifteen bishops, or one bishop for every thirty graduates.

Today, of the 525 living graduates, it is still true that the great majority are hard at work as pastors and community leaders. It may also be noted that twelve are now deans of cathedrals, thirteen are headmasters of schools, two are presidents of colleges, and twenty-four are bishops, or one bishop for every twenty-two graduates. That this proportion is larger than might normally be expected is evident when we consider that of the 6300 clergy in the Church at large, 144 are bishops, or one out of forty-three. The School's Alumni, while numbering but one-twelfth of the Church's clergy, supply one-sixth of its episcopate.

There is something almost ironical in the fact that a school which has no bishop on its governing board and whose early leaders were insistent that none ever be put there has contributed so generously to the personnel of the episcopate.

"The School has never properly appreciated bishops," drolly remarked Bishop Atwood of Arizona at an Alumni gathering. "At the Commencement following my consecration, after I had been knocked about by old friends and stood somewhat neglected in a corner while an English visitor kindly talked to me as a poor missionary from the southwest, a young alumnus addressed me as Bishop. 'What,' said the Englishman, 'is it possible you are a bishop of the Church? It is astounding how they treat a bishop here.' 'Yes,' I said, 'it is.' "

Despite this astounding treatment, alumni have not only become bishops, they have become archbishops! Shahe Vartabed Kasparian, '16, became an archbishop in the Armenian Church as well as head of the theological seminary at Antilyas, Syria. James DeWolf Perry, '94, became Presiding Bishop of the American Church.

In addition to bishoprics and rectorships, deanships and headmasterships, alumni are filling other positions of leadership. The Assessor to the present Presiding Bishop is an alumnus, as are the Promotional Chairman of the Forward Movement, the Chairman and the Executive Secretary of the Army and Navy Commission, the Administrative Vice-President of the National Council, the Associate Foreign Secretary and the Assistant Domestic Secretary of the Department of Missions. Twenty alumni are professors or instructors in theological schools. Alumni are chaplains of St. Luke's Hospital, New York, and of the Massachusetts General Hospital, Boston. The General Secretary of the Yale Christian Association is an alumnus, and alumni are either official university chaplains or chaplains to Episcopal students at Harvard, Princeton, Cornell, Michigan, Brown, Bates, Wellesley, the University of Pennsylvania, Pennsylvania State College, Ohio State, the University of Iowa, the University of Missouri, Leland Stanford, St. John's University, Shanghai, St. Paul's University, Tokyo, and St. Mary's College, Raleigh. Forty-two have become chaplains in the army or navy, and others are making application for appointment.

Conditions in the Far East have made the temporary return of many missionaries imperative, but until very recently twenty-four alumni were serving in distant lands and two more are under appointment for such service, to be sent out on cessation of hostilities. Even under present conditions alumni are at work in India, Liberia, Japan, the Philippine Islands, occupied and unoccupied China, Panama, and Alaska. They are also at work at home in forty-one states and in Canada.

Whether at home or abroad, whether in the high councils of the Church or in the humblest rural community, wherever they are exercising a genuine ministry they are, as Dean Hodges once put it, "the exceeding great reward of their teachers."

What the future holds for them and for the School we dare not prophesy, but we may repeat with assurance the words of Bishop Lawrence, spoken at a similar moment in the School's history, at its fiftieth anniversary: "*Watchman, what of the night?* God only knows. Let this stand sure. The same forces that have made this School must be sustained to perpetuate it: truth and life, reality, vigor, and leadership, such faith, living and moving in us as will give perfect confidence in Christ."

BOOKS WRITTEN BY PAST AND PRESENT MEMBERS OF THE FACULTY

FRANCIS WHARTON

Since each of the editions of Wharton's books represent a substantial revision and enlargement, a few of these revisions, including the last in each case, are noted. Those after his death are bracketed.

A Treatise on the Criminal Law of the United States. 1846. Expanded to 2 vols. in 5th edition, 1861. [12th edition, 1932.]

Precedents of Indictments and Pleas. 1849. Expanded to 2 vols. in 3rd edition, 1871. 4th edition, 1881.

State Trials of the United States during the Administrations of Washington and Adams. 1849.

A Treatise on the Law of Homicide. 1855. [3rd edition, 1907.]

A Treatise on Medical Jurisprudence (with Moreton Stillé). 1855. Expanded to 2 vols. in 3rd edition, 1873. [5th edition, 1905.]

A Letter to the Rt. Rev. H. W. Lee, D.D., Bishop of the Diocese of Iowa, on the Present Condition of the Domestic Missions of the Protestant Episcopal Church. 1858.

The Missouri Valley and Lay Preaching. 1859.

A Treatise on Theism and on the Modern Skeptical Theories. 1859.

The Silence of Scripture. 1867.

A Treatise on the Conflict of Laws. 1872. [3rd edition, 1905.]

A Treatise on the Law of Negligence. 1874. 2nd edition, 1878.

A Commentary on the Law of Agency and Agents. 1876.

A Commentary on the Law of Evidence in Civil Issues. 2 vols. 1877. 3rd edition, 1888.

Philosophy of Criminal Law. 1880.

A Treatise on the Law of Evidence in Criminal Issues. 1880 (expanded from material previously in *A Treatise on the Criminal Law*). [11th edition, 1935.]

A Treatise on Criminal Pleading and Practice. 1880 (expanded from material previously in *A Treatise on the Criminal Law*). [10th edition, 1918.]

Retributive Justice. 1882.

A Commentary on the Law of Contracts. 2 vols. 1882.

Commentaries on Law . . . International . . . Constitutional and Statutory. 1884.

A Digest of the International Law of the United States. 3 vols. 1886.

The Revolutionary Diplomatic Correspondence of the United States. 6 vols. 1889.

JOHN SEELY STONE

Lectures to Sabbath School Teachers on Mental Cultivation. 1839.

Memoir of the Life of the Rt. Rev. Alexander Viets Griswold. 1844.

Lectures on the Institution of the Sabbath. 1844. Revised and republished as *The Divine Rest.* 1867.

The Mysteries Opened. 1844. Revised and republished as *The Christian Sacraments.* 1866.

The Church Universal. 1846. Revised and republished as *The Living Temple.* 1866.

A Memoir of the Life of James Milnor. 1848. Abridged. 1849.

The Contrast, or the Evangelical and Tractarian Systems Compared. 1853.

A Discourse Commemorative of the Life and Character of the Rev. James May. 1864.

PETER HENRY STEENSTRA

Translation of Lange's *Commentary on Judges and Ruth.* 1872.

The Being of God as Unity and Trinity. 1891.

ALEXANDER VIETS GRISWOLD ALLEN

The Continuity of Christian Thought. 1884. A new edition, 1894. [Another, 1930.]

Jonathan Edwards. 1889.

Religious Progress. 1894.

Christian Institutions. 1897.

Life and Letters of Phillips Brooks. 2 vols. 1900.
Phillips Brooks. 1907.
Freedom in the Church. 1907.

GEORGE ZABRISKIE GRAY
  The Children's Crusade. 1870.
  The Scriptural Doctrine of Recognition in the World to Come.
    1875.
  Husband and Wife. 1885.
  The Church's Certain Faith. 1890.

ELISHA MULFORD
  The Nation. 1870 [reprinted 1894].
  The Republic of God. 1881.

HENRY SYLVESTER NASH
  Genesis of the Social Conscience. 1897.
  Ethics and Revelation. 1899.
  The History of the Higher Criticism of the New Testament.
    1900. New edition, 1906.
  The Atoning Life. 1908.
  Prayers and Meditations. 1915.

WILLIAM LAWRENCE
  Life of Amos A. Lawrence. 1888.
  Visions and Service. 1896.
  Roger Wolcott. 1902.
  Phillips Brooks, A Study. 1903.
  The American Cathedral. 1919.
  Fifty Years. 1923.
  Henry Cabot Lodge. 1925.
  Memories of a Happy Life. 1926.
  Life of Phillips Brooks. 1930.
  Seventy-three Years of the Episcopal Theological School. 1940.

MAXIMILIAN LINDSAY KELLNER
  The Prophecies of Isaiah. 1895.
  The Standard Inscription of Asshurnazirpal. 1895.

The Assyrian Monuments Illustrating the Sermons of Isaiah. 1900.

The History of the Hebrews. 1901.

The History of Old Testament Literature and Religion. 1902.

EDWARD STAPLES DROWN

The Apostles' Creed Today. 1917.

God's Responsibility for the War. 1919.

The Creative Christ. 1922.

Religion or God. 1927.

GEORGE HODGES

The Church Catechism in Forty Lessons. 1884.

The Creed, the Ten Commandments, and the Lord's Prayer in Forty Lessons. 1885.

Beside the Cross. 1890.

The Episcopal Church, Its Doctrine, Ministry, Discipline, Worship, and Sacraments. 1892.

Christianity between Sundays. 1892.

The Heresy of Cain. 1894.

Faith and Social Service. 1896.

In this Present World. 1897.

Battles of Peace. 1899.

The Path of Life. 1900.

William Penn. 1901.

Fountains Abbey. 1904.

The Human Nature of the Saints. 1904.

When the King Came. 1904.

The Cross and Passion. 1904.

Three Hundred Years of the Episcopal Church in America. 1906.

The Pursuit of Happiness. 1906.

The Year of Grace. 1906.

The Happy Family. 1906.

The Administration of an Institutional Church (with John Reichert). 1906.

Holderness. 1907.

The Apprenticeship of Washington. 1909.

The Garden of Eden. 1909.

The Training of Children in Religion. 1911.

A Child's Guide to the Bible. 1911.

Everyman's Religion. 1911.

Saints and Heroes. 2 vols. 1911-12.

The Castle of Zion. 1912.

Moral Training in the School and Home (with E. H. Sneath). 1913.

The Golden Rule Readers (with E. H. Sneath and E. L. Stevens). 6 vols. 1913.

A Classbook of Old Testament History. 1914.

The Early Church. 1915.

The Episcopal Church, Its Faith and Order. 1915. [Revised edition, 1932.]

Henry Codman Potter. 1915.

The King's Highway Readers (with E. H. Sneath and H. H. Tweedy). 8 vols. 1916.

Religious Training in the School and Home (with E. H. Sneath and H. H. Tweedy). 1917.

Religion in a World at War. 1917.

How to Know the Bible. 1918.

PHILIP MERCER RHINELANDER

The Things Most Surely Believed among Us. 1916.

The Faith of the Cross. 1916.

The Gospel of the Kingdom. 1917.

Religion in War Time. 1918.

Think Out Your Faith. 1926.

HENRY BRADFORD WASHBURN

Men of Conviction. 1931.

The Religious Motive in Philanthropy. 1931.

SAMUEL McCOMB

Religion and Medicine (with E. Worcester and I. H. Coriat). 1908.

The Making of the English Bible. 1909.

The Power of Self-Suggestion. 1909.

The Christian Religion as a Healing Power (with E. Worcester). 1909.

Christianity and the Modern Mind. 1910.

A Book of Prayers for Public and Personal Use. 1912. Enlarged, 1923.

Prayer: What It Is and What It Does. 1913.

Faith. 1915.

The New Life. 1917.

God's Meaning in Life. 1917.

Prayers for Today. 1918.

The Future Life in the Light of Modern Inquiry. 1919.

The Power of Prayer. 1921.

A Book of Modern Prayers. 1926.

Preaching in Theory and Practice. 1926.

Body, Mind, and Spirit (with E. Worcester). 1931.

Translation of Friedrich Heiler's *Prayer* (with J. E. Park). 1932.

JAMES THAYER ADDISON

The Story of the First Gas Regiment. 1919.

Chinese Ancestor Worship. 1925.

Our Father's Business. 1927.

Francis Xavier. 1929.

François Coillard. 1929.

Our Expanding Church. 1930. Revised, 1935.

Life Beyond Death in the Beliefs of Mankind. 1932. French translation by R. Godet, 1936.

The Way of Christ. 1934. Chinese translation by F. L. H. Pott, 1939.

The Medieval Missionary. 1936.

The Lord's Prayer. 1937.

Parables of Our Lord. 1940.

The Christian Approach to the Moslem. 1942.

WILLIAM HENRY PAINE HATCH

The Pauline Idea of Faith. 1917.

The Gospel Manuscripts of the General Theological Seminary (with C. C. Edmunds). 1918.

The Idea of Faith in Christian Literature. 1925.

Greek and Syrian Miniatures in Jerusalem. 1931.

The Greek Manuscripts of the New Testament at Mount Sinai. 1932.

The Greek Manuscripts of the New Testament in Jerusalem. 1934.

The "Western" Text of the Gospels. 1937.

The Principal Uncial Manuscripts of the New Testament. 1939.

An Album of Dated Syriac Manuscripts. 1943.

Facsimiles and Descriptions of Minuscule Manuscripts of the New Testament. 1943.

JAMES ARTHUR MULLER

Stephen Gardiner and the Tudor Reaction. 1926.

Revised edition of Hodges' *The Episcopal Church, Its Faith and Order.* 1932.

The Letters of Stephen Gardiner. 1933.

Apostle of China. 1937. Chinese translation by H. S. Wei. 1940.

The Episcopal Theological School, 1867–1943. 1943.

ANGUS DUN

Religion among American Men. 1920.

The King's Cross. 1926.

We Believe. 1934.

The Meanings of Unity. 1937.

Studies in Church Unity. 1938.

Not by Bread Alone. 1942.

SHERMAN ELBRIDGE JOHNSON

Beginner's Manual of New Testament Greek (with A. H. Forster). 1936.

Translation of Johannes Weiss' *History of Primitive Christianity* (with three others). 2 vols. 1937.

MASSEY HAMILTON SHEPHERD, JR.

History of St. James' Church, Chicago. 1934.

A Short History of Christianity (with five others). 1940.

ADELAIDE TEAGUE CASE
  Liberal Christianity and Religious Education. 1924.
  As Modern Writers See Jesus. 1927.
  Seven Psalms. 1935.
  The Servant of the Lord. 1940.

WASHBURN, HATCH, McCOMB, MULLER, ADDISON, N. B. NASH, DUN
  Creeds and Loyalty. 1924.

INSTRUCTORS AND PART-TIME LECTURERS

In many instances, especially in the fields of Theology, Missions, Religious Education, and Pastoral Care, the instruction given ran through only a part of the academic year indicated.

IN PREACHING

Henry Codman Potter	1867–68
Charles Morris Addison	1919–20
Philo Woodruff Sprague	1919–20
Henry Knox Sherrill	1926–29
Henry Martyn Medary	1927–28
Philemon Fowler Sturges	1927–40
Raymond Calkins	1929–32, 1940–41
Charles Leslie Glenn	1932–36
Phillips Endecott Osgood	1934–
Boynton Merrill	1940–42
Edwin Jan van Etten	1940–42
Gardiner Mumford Day	1941–43
Theodore Parker Ferris	1943–

IN THEOLOGY

John McCrady	1876–77
Alexander Hamilton Vinton	1877–81
Elisha Mulford	1882–85
Frederic Dan Huntington	1889–90
H. Richard Harris	1889–90
John Steinfort Kedney	1890–91
Charles A. L. Richards	1890–91
William Reed Huntington	1890–91
William Alexander	1891–92
Stewart Means	1891–92
Charles James Wood	1891–92
George Lyman Paine	1903–04
Paul Johannes Tillich	1938–39
John Daniel Wild	1938–39
Helmut Richard Niebuhr	1940–41
Clement William Welsh	1941–42

In Polity and Canon Law

Reginald Heber Howe	1881–82
Joseph Cullen Ayer	1900–05
John Wallace Suter	1915–16
Theodore Russell Ludlow	1922–23

In Voice

Henry Dixon Jones	1888–89
James E. Murdoch	1889–90
H. P. Townsend	1889–90
John Joseph Hayes	1890–99
William Edward Gardner	1899–1900
Sarah H. Hooker	1899–1901
Charles Townsend Copeland	1900–01
Charles Adams Allen	1901–08
William Alden Paul	1900–01, 1908–17
Irvah Lester Winter	1917–18
Richard Gilmore Appel	1918–21
May Sleeper Ruggles	1921–38
Robert Clyde Yarbrough	1938–40
Frank Zacher	1940–43
Clifton Lunt	1943–

In Sociology

Frederick Baylies Allen	1894–95
Robert Archey Woods	1895–1914
Percy Gamble Kammerer	1917–22

In the History of Religion and Missions

Edward Abbott	1899–1900
James Haughton Woods	1899–1900, 1906–07
William Edward Gardner	1911–12
Duncan Black Macdonald	1911–12
James Bishop Thomas	1911–12
Elwood Worcester	1911–12
Frederick Wells Williams	1912–13
Charles Henry Brent	1913–14
Hugh Latimer Burleson	1914–15
Logan Herbert Roots	1916–17
Arthur Romeyn Gray	1917–18
Ronald Owen Hall	1941–42
Basil Joseph Mathews	1942–43

In New Testament

Joseph Henry Thayer	1900–01

William Henry Ryder	1912–13
Kirsopp Lake	1913–14
MacKinley Helm	1930–33
John Russell Dallinger	1934–37
Oscar Jacob Frank Seitz	1937–40
Ernest Findlay Scott	1939–40

IN CHURCH HISTORY

John Wallace Suter	1901–02
Daniel Dulany Addison	1917–18

IN MUSIC

Ernest Douglas	1901–02
John Wallace Goodrich	1904–05
Richard Gilmore Appel	1914–22, 1925–
Arthur Vincent Bennett	1922–25
Walter Williams	1937–39
Ludwig Theis	1940–41

IN OLD TESTAMENT

Harry Leroy Taylor	1907–08
Royden Keith Yerkes	1922–23
Fleming James	1923–24
Henry Joel Cadbury	1924–26

IN LITURGICS

John Wallace Suter	1911–12, 1920–22

IN RELIGIOUS EDUCATION

Frederic Curtiss Lauderburn	1912–13
John Wallace Suter, Jr.	1919–25
William Edward Gardner	1923–24, 1925–27
Cyril Edward Hudson	1927–28
Theodore Gerald Soares	1927–28
Robert Seneca Smith	1927–28
William Murray Bradner	1930–31
Erna B. Blaydow	1934–37
Mildred Hewitt	1934–37
Charles Frederick Lancaster	1935–36, 1937–40

IN PASTORAL CARE

Philo Woodruff Sprague	1915–16, 1919–20
Charles Morris Addison	1919–20
William Lawrence	1923–29
Ernest Joseph Dennen	1923–32
Richard Clarke Cabot	1924–25, 1926–27

Alfred Worcester   1924–25, 1926–28
Eugene L. Emerson   1926–27
Philip Mercer Rhinelander   1926–27
William Healy   1926–32
Charles Lewis Slattery   1927–28
Anton Boisen   1927–28
John Thomas Dallas   1927–28
Albert Warren Stearns   1927–28
Elwood Worcester   1927–28
Henry Wise Hobson   1927–29
William Appleton Lawrence   1927–29
Willard Learoyd Sperry   1927–29
Douglas Thom   1927–30
Charles Macfie Campbell   1927–32
Spence Burton   1928–30
Elton Mayo   1929–31
Otis Radcliffe Rice   1929–32
Henry Knox Sherrill   1929–32
Benjamin Martin Washburn   1931–32
Gordon Willard Allport   1934–35
Jacob Clemens Kolb   1934–35
Richard Tuttle Loring   1934–35
Russell Dicks   1935–36
Arthur Carl Lichtenberger   1935–41
Cornelius Polhemus Trowbridge   1936–37
David Robert Hunter   1937–42
Frederic Cunningham Lawrence   1941–
Rollin Jonathan Fairbanks   1942–

BIBLIOGRAPHY

I

Manuscripts, Typescripts, and Scrapbooks in the School
Archives:

A large collection of letters from and to trustees, deans, professors, and alumni.

Trustees' minutes.

Visitors' minutes.

Faculty minutes.

Minutes of student societies.

Faculty reports to Trustees (for the years 1885–96, 1898–1930 these are also in print).

Treasurers' reports.

A. V. G. Allen's notes on School's history.

A. V. G. Allen's sermon on Dr. Mulford.

Stenographic report of Alumni banquet at School's fiftieth anniversary, 1907.

A volume of Dean Hodges' notes on School affairs, 1901–09.

A volume of Dean Hodges' notes on "Precedents and Customs," 1904–14.

Q. M. Wilder's thesis on H. S. Nash.

Scrapbook of clippings on election of Bishop Paddock and Nathan Matthews' offer of $100,000 to the School in 1873.

Scrapbook of pamphlets and notices concerning the School, 1877–87, collected by Dean Gray.

Scrapbook of clippings, programs, and notices concerning Dean Gray, Dean Lawrence, and the School, 1884–93, collected by Dean Lawrence.

Scrapbook of clippings and pamphlets on "the Massachusetts Case" and the Pastoral Letter, 1894, collected by Dean Hodges.

II

Manuscript Material not in the School Archives:
Dean Hodges' journal (a combination diary and scrapbook). 33 vols. 1881–1907. In possession of Mrs. Hodges.
A Book of Remembrance, containing letters from 420 alumni to Dean Washburn in 1940. 2 vols. In possession of Dean Washburn.
A few letters on the affiliation with Harvard. In the Harvard archives.

III

Publications of the Episcopal Theological School:
Annual *Catalogue*, 1868 to present.
Official Bulletin (and its Supplements) four times a year, 1909 to present.
Annual letters *To the Friends of the Episcopal Theological School*. 1929 to present.
Indenture [of B. T. Reed]. 1867.
Indentures [of B. T. Reed and R. M. Mason, 1868].
Consecration of St. John's Memorial Chapel. 1870.
A Statement of the Trustees . . . to which is appended the Correspondence between them and Mr. Nathan Matthews. 1873.
Act of Incorporation and By-Laws. 1874.
Summary of the Records of the Trustees. 1887.
Charter and By-Laws. 1904.
Fundamental Articles, Charter, By-Laws, and Officers. 1911.
Of the School in Cambridge. (Endowment Campaign booklet). [1922.]

IV

Other Books, Pamphlets, and Articles (N.B. Titles given in the text or in the list of books by the Faculty are not repeated here):
Allen, A. V. G. A letter on his life at college and the influence of Dr. Wharton, in G. F. Smythe, *Kenyon College*. New Haven, 1924. P. 178.
"Elisha Mulford," in *Christian Union*, March 11, 1886.

Brooks, P. *Alexander Hamilton Vinton, A Memorial Sermon.* Boston, 1881.

Church Militant, The. Boston. Frequent news items and articles about the School and persons connected with it; notably in issues of April, 1902, April, 1903, October, 1903, April, 1904, May, 1904, March, 1907, May, 1907, May, 1920, May, 1942.

Clark, T. M. *Reminiscences.* New York, 1895.

Fletcher, H. H. *A History of the Church of Our Saviour in Longwood, Massachusetts.* Brookline, 1936.

Gray, G. Z. "The Episcopal Theological School," in W. S. Perry, *The History of the American Episcopal Church.* Boston, 1885. Vol. II, p. 535.
　　Henry W. Longfellow. A Memorial Sermon. [Cambridge?] 1882.
　　John S. Stone, D.D. A Memorial Sermon. [Cambridge? 1882.]

Hodges, G. *The Religion of a Seminarian.* An address. New York, 1906.
　　Seminaries and Subscriptions. A sermon. Cambridge, 1903.

Hodges, J. S. *George Hodges.* New York, 1926.

Hopkins, J. H. Jr. *The Life of the Late Rt. Rev. John Henry Hopkins.* New York, 1873.

Journals of the Conventions of the Protestant Episcopal Church in the Diocese of Massachusetts, 1784–1828. Boston, 1849. The same for 1829 and years following, published annually.

Lawrence, W. *George Zabriskie Gray, D.D. A Memorial Sermon.* Boston, 1890.
　　"Memoir of Amos Adams Lawrence," in *Proceedings of the Massachusetts Historical Society.* December, 1897, and January, 1898.
　　"Personal Notes on a Campaign" [for E.T.S. endowment], in *Christian Education,* New York, May, 1923.
　　"Recollections of Early Boston Churchmen," in *Boston Evening Transcript,* July 2, 1927.

Mann, A. *In Memory of Robert Treat Paine. A Sermon.* [Boston] 1911.

Melish, J. H. *Franklin Spencer Spalding.* New York, 1917.

Moore, J. B. *A Sketch of the Life of Francis Wharton.* In Wharton, *The Revolutionary Diplomatic Correspondence of the United States.* Washington, 1891.

Moulton, A. W. *A Memoir of Augustine Heard Amory.* Salem, 1909.

Muller, J. A. "George Hodges, Popularizer of Church History," in *Historical Magazine of the Protestant Episcopal Church.* March, 1940.

Nash, H. S. *Alexander Viets Griswold Allen, D.D.* A memorial sermon. Cambridge, 1908.
"The Episcopal Theological School," in *The Churchman.* June 26, 1886.

Packard, J. *Recollections of a Long Life.* Washington, 1902.

Robbins, H. C. *Charles Lewis Slattery.* New York, 1931.
The New Theology. A sermon. [New York] 1917.

Wells, C. L. "Memoir of Alexander Viets Griswold Allen," in *Proceedings of the Massachusetts Historical Society.* January, 1911.

Wharton, F. "Church Parties as Apologists," in *Bibliotheca Sacra*, July, 1880.

[Wharton, H. A.] *Francis Wharton, A Memoir.* Philadelphia, 1891.

Winthrop, R. C., Jr. *Memoir of Robert C. Winthrop.* Boston, 1897.
Memoir of Robert M. Mason. Cambridge, 1881.

Biographical sketches of many persons connected with the School are found in *Appleton's Cyclopedia of American Biography*, *Dictionary of American Biography*, and *Who's Who in America*.

INDEX

INDEX